THE
ANDEAN
COSMOVISION

THE
ANDEAN
COSMOVISION

A Path for Exploring Profound Aspects
of Ourselves, Nature, and the Cosmos

Oakley E. Gordon, Ph.D.

ISBN: 978-0-9904800-0-6

Interior and cover design: Kubera Book Design

www.SalkaWind.com
info@SalkaWind.com

TABLE OF CONTENTS

INTRODUCTION

This is a guidebook. It is not a philosophy book (although there is a little bit of philosophy in it), nor is it primarily a description of the Andean way of understanding reality (although there is a fair amount of description in it). It is instead a guide to help you explore new facets of yourself, of Nature, and of the Cosmos. I can't describe what you will find. You will need to go there and discover that for yourself. I can say that this is a path with a heart, that it will touch the part of you that delights in beauty and laughter, that it is an adventure, and that it nourishes a more loving and mutually supportive relationship between yourself and Nature and the Cosmos.

You don't need a guru for this path. You need the Pachamama (the great Being who is the mother earth), you need the Apus (the great Beings who are the majestic mountain peaks), you need the stars, the wind, the trees, the rivers, the sun. This book can only open the door to new territory and give you a map and some advice. It is up to you to determine whether what you find is in harmony with your deepest values. If this path touches something beautiful deep inside of you, then keep going, it only gets better.

For the past twenty years, I have been exploring the Andean way of experiencing reality (which I call the *Andean Cosmovision*) under the tutelage of my Peruvian mentor and friend don Américo Yábar. In my trips to Peru don Américo has also arranged for me to work with numerous other paqos (Andean mystics/shamans) including his son, Gayle Yábar. From don

Américo and the other paqos I have learned how to explore the Andean Cosmovision but most of the actual exploration of this Cosmovision has occurred while I have been back home in the United States.

I have come to realize there are two aspects to this path. One aspect is to learn how to experience reality through the Andean Cosmovision; this is what I have learned in Peru. The second aspect is to figure out how to integrate this experience of reality into our lives here in the modern, Western world. This integration is something that the Andean people can't teach us. It is up to us to discover how to do it. My intent in writing this book is to help you do both.

The heart of the book are the "how to" bits, where I lay out the various experiential processes that serve as the doorway for exploring these new facets of reality. These bits are woven into a larger tapestry of thoughts and concepts that support the experiences and that help us to integrate what we learn into our Western view of reality. The Andean Cosmovision moves us into a dance with the vast ineffable mystery of the Cosmos. There is no linear way of proceeding, yet words and thoughts (and books) are linear. I recommend that you read the chapters in the order they are given, as some of the later chapters assume you have read some of the earlier chapters. If you continue to use this book as a guide, however, then you can always come back to reread just the chapters you need at that time. That is how I use this material.

THE ANDEAN COSMOVISION

Indescribable...but not imperceptible.

The Andean Cosmovision provides a path for exploring profound aspects of ourselves, Nature, and the Cosmos[1]. It has its roots in the indigenous culture of the Andes of South America where it informs the lives of people who live in isolated villages, high in the mountains, far from the nearest road.[2] In our modern, Western culture it resonates with people who are drawn to its simplicity, its beauty, and the loving connection it nourishes between ourselves and Nature and the Cosmos.

The term *Cosmovision* refers to a way of understanding and relating to reality. The Andean Cosmovision is not intellectual in nature. It is not a set of ideas or beliefs. It simply cannot be defined, described, or encompassed with word or thought. It can, however, be experienced and it can be explored. Eventually you come to understand the Cosmovision, but this understanding is not intellectual, it is an understanding that develops at a deeper level of your Being. The two most important aspects of this exploration are the various meditative-like processes with which you explore reality, and the relationship with Nature and the Cosmos that the meditations nourish.

This path is one of experiential exploration. The experiences come from trying out various experiential processes that I label as meditations. They are not exactly meditations, that is just the closest term I can come up with in English to describe them. They are ways of changing our experience of reality. You will see what I mean when you get to the chapters that describe the meditations. After a meditation, you evaluate its effect on you and then decide whether or not to include it in your repertoire of ways to face the vast mystery and beauty of existence. In our mechanistic, reductionistic, technoistic (I made that word up) society we rarely attend to the mystery and beauty of the Cosmos and of our existence within it, but this is exactly the territory that the Andean Cosmovision gives us the tools and guidance to explore.

There is no moral imperative within the Andean Cosmovision that this path should be pursued. It is not a matter of shoulds and shouldn'ts. It is a matter of harmony and beauty. You are the ultimate authority for what a meditation accomplishes and whether or not it has value to you. If you like the effect of the meditation, then incorporate it into your life, if not then move on to another meditation or to a different path. It is my experience that no path works for everyone.

There are also more beautiful and deeper effects that slowly emerge as we continue down this path. These arise naturally from the way the meditations change our relationship with Nature and the Cosmos. The meditations nourish a more loving and mutually supportive relationship with Nature and the Cosmos. It is a relationship that is not conceivable within the Western view of reality. From this relationship, new facets of our existence and new aspects of Nature and the Cosmos come into our awareness. Following the path provided by the Andean Cosmovision leads to a sense of our belonging in the Cosmos and to a heartfelt appreciation of Nature. There also arises a strong sense that this path is not just for our benefit alone, but is also beneficial to (and appreciated by) Nature and the Cosmos as well.

— ENDNOTES —

[1] According to my Webster's dictionary the terms *Nature* and the *Cosmos* are essentially synonymous. When I use the terms, however, *Nature* refers to that part of the Cosmos that is immediate and dear to me, including the trees under which I sit, the earth (Pachamama), the sky, and the river flowing by. I use the term *Cosmos* to refer to everything: Nature as defined above, as well as the sun (Tai Tai Inti), the stars, the moon (Mama Killa), and the void (Mama Tuta) that holds them all in her embrace. I also choose to capitalize Nature and the Cosmos and a few other terms (e.g., Being) out of respect and deep fondness, and to give them a higher status than they normally have in our everyday world.

[2] In this book I present a collection of concepts and beliefs that support the "how-to" aspect of the Andean Cosmovision. While I call it the *Andean* Cosmovision, the details of the concepts and beliefs vary great across the Andes. These differences are important to anthropologists, and rightly so, for it is important to know which areas of the Andes believe what, and it is interesting to study how differences in beliefs may have come about. From the viewpoint of wanting to have a Cosmovision that we can use to explore the territory, however, these differences are not important. They are but different guide books to the same territory, and ultimately it is the territory that matters. I am writing this guidebook from my own adventures and explorations, based upon the advice and help of my teachers in Peru (primarily don Américo Yábar). The details reflect the Cosmovision of my particular teachers and their expression comes through me, a child of the West. I would like to think, however, that if you shared this guidebook with any paqo (mystic/shaman) of the Andes that they would at least say that the descriptions sound vaguely familiar.

BAREFOOT IN THE MOUNTAINS

From a song sung to me in Quechua by women of the high Andes.

I walk without shoes in the mountains.
My bare feet touch the mountain.
The mountain takes pleasure in knowing my body.

Apu Ausangate, Peru. Photo taken at 15,000 feet.

The Andean people live in a world where the mountains, the trees, the rivers are as aware of the people as the people are of them.

THE CRAZY ANIMAL

We humans have all the technology we need to turn this planet into a garden of Eden—a planet abundant with a diversity of life, healthy and unpolluted with little disease, hunger, and poverty. Sometimes in my despair over the current state of the world and our apparent trajectory, I forget the very good news that we actually have the tools we need to create such a beautiful future. We also, however, have the choice to move toward the mass extinction of species, the destruction of all the beautiful places on the planet, and increasing pollution, famine, war, poverty, and misery. Given these two choices, why does our species appear to favor the second option? It seems like such an incredibly stupid and crazy thing to do. I believe that the answer to that question can be found in the assumptions that underlie our Western culture.

A culture, or an individual for that matter, cannot operate without some assumptions about the basic nature of the way things are. Assumptions are interesting things. They are rarely brought to the light of day to be examined because, well, they are assumed to be true. Every culture has a set of assumptions about the nature of reality. These assumptions make it possible for that culture to excel at some things while at the same time making it hard for the culture to be good at other things.

My Western, industrial culture has a set of assumptions about the nature of the Cosmos that make us really good at inventing technology. Technology has given us so many things that enhance our lives: personal computers, telephones, electric lights, hot water at the turn of a tap, furnaces to keep our houses

5

warm, and refrigerators to keep our perishable food cool. The assumptions, however, that make us so good at technology also make it difficult for us to do certain other things well. We find it difficult as a society, for example, to live in harmony with the rest of life on this planet.

The default setting in our society—what we need to pay attention to and the behaviors we need to do to get by in our daily lives—separates us from our connection to the rest of nature. This in turn leads us to engage in behaviors that are killing our planet, and time is running out for us to change our ways. It is as if we are sitting in the backseat of a car playing with (and fighting over) our toys while the car speeds towards a cliff. When we shoot off the edge of that cliff it will be too late to do anything about it, and we will take much of what is beautiful in this world with us.

The traditional Andean culture has a different set of assumptions about the nature of reality (what I call the Andean Cosmovision). These assumptions nourish a mutually supportive relationship between the Andean people and Nature, a relationship that is difficult to conceive of, let alone attain, within the view of reality held by my Western culture. The default setting for the traditional Andean culture—what they pay attention to and what they need to do to get by in their daily lives—reinforces their experience of being connected with Nature and the rest of the Cosmos. The assumptions that connect them with the beauty and the sacredness of Nature, however, make it difficult for them to excel in other ways. I doubt, for example, that the Andean culture—had its evolution not been halted by the Spanish conquistadors—would have ever gotten around to inventing the internal combustion engine.

My culture has the knowledge and technology we need to head for a future of great beauty on this planet but apparently we lack the heart to do so. The Andean culture has the heart. For a future of beauty to be possible I believe we need to integrate the two world views.

The path I am proposing does not involve just learning the Andean Cosmovision but also discovering how to integrate it into our lives here in modern Western culture. The Andeans can't teach us the latter. That is up to us and is one of the great contributions we can make toward a more beautiful future for this planet. When I first started going to Peru, almost twenty years ago, I would return and have a very difficult time entering back into my everyday life. In Peru my Western view of reality seemed like an illusion, and when I was back in the U.S. my Peruvian experiences would slowly fade into the status of having been but pleasant dreams. I felt that I could be one way (Andean) or another (Western), but there was no connection between the two. It was as if I were less than the sum of these two parts. Slowly, over the years, I began to integrate the two ways of being in the world. My intent with this book is to help you both explore the Andean Cosmovision and integrate it into your life. The Andean Cosmovision is beautiful in its own right, the integration even more.

PAQO: SHAMAN OR MYSTIC?

My work in Peru has been with the paqos who live in the high Andes. The term *paqo* (sometimes spelled *paq'o*) does not have an exact equivalent in our culture. Some people translate it as *shaman* and others as *mystic*. Neither one is a particularly great choice. It is like trying to describe a bear to someone who has never seen one and having to choose between saying it is somewhat like a large cat or somewhat like a large dog.

The word *shaman* comes from the indigenous culture of Siberia where it refers to people who have special powers and a corresponding special role in their society. The term has since been adopted by our Western culture and applied to people with similar roles and powers in cultures across the globe. While this has diluted the meaning of the term, still there are basic elements to being a shaman. Shamans typically enter into altered states of consciousness through the use of psychoactive plants, drumming, or chanting. While in these states they may journey into spirit realms not normally accessible in everyday

A Siberian Shaman: Smithsonian

life, and there they gather information or take actions to heal people whose afflictions have their root in these spirit realms. The role of the shaman in society centers around this ability to perform these special deeds.

Mystics, on the other hand, are those who seek to know through direct experience the essential, sacred nature of the Cosmos. Our thoughts, concepts, and sensory perception, are interpretations of reality, not reality itself. The experience, for example, that we are separate entities moving through time is a product of our mind. It is our experience of reality after the mind has translated it into something that makes sense, it is not the essential 'suchness' of reality itself. When we experience reality before our mind has a chance to interpret it we find an eternal, seamless whole, and we find the sacred. This place of deep knowing is the goal of the mystic.

Paqos have some of the attributes of both shamans and mystics. The paqos are like mystics in that they nourish an inter-active and mutually supportive relationship with the rest of the Cosmos, a relationship that is only possible through the direct experience of the interconnectedness of all things. Paqos differ from traditional mystics, however, in that mystics tend to be soli-tary figures who may have found it necessary to withdraw from society to pursue their path of knowledge. To be a paqo is to be of service both to the great Beings of Nature and the Cosmos and to the community. This service is always performed within the context of *ayni*, the Andean principle of reciprocity, where giving is balanced by receiving and receiving is balanced by giv-ing. I'll have a lot more to say about ayni in later chapters.

Like shamans, the paqos have abilities that fall outside the ken of our culture's conceptions of reality. These abilities, how-ever, are not "powers"; they involve neither controlling Nature nor being controlled by Nature (i.e., neither mastery nor servi-tude). They stem instead from having a mutually supportive and loving relationship with the rest of the Cosmos.

Andean Paqos: Photo by Elaine Nichols

Paqos are not exactly shamans or mystics, or they are both. If forced to choose (to avoid long explanations) I usually go with mystic, and thus I label what I am studying as Andean mysticism rather than Andean shamanism. Few people would know what I meant if I called it Andean paqoism and I am reluctant to be held responsible for introducing a term like paqoism into our world.

WHY A SWAN?

Our intellect is a very important part of our existence. Its main task is to determine what is true and what is false. This is the goal of both science and Western religion. There are, however, times when this process is irrelevant and even gets in our way.

Let us consider a performance of the ballet Swan Lake. A ballerina appears on the stage dressed as a swan. This is not the appropriate context for the scientist to leap up and shout, "Don't be fooled, that is not really a swan!"; nor is it appropriate for a priest to stand up and exclaim, "Look, a giant swan. It's a miracle!" On the other side of the relationship the ballerina does not stop upon entering the stage to announce, "Please do not be fooled, I am not really a swan"; nor does she announce, "It is important that you believe that I truly am a swan." These considerations are appropriate in the correct contexts, but there are times when something of value is going on and the judgments of the scientist and the priest are simply not relevant. There are times, in other words, when being either skeptical or gullible gets in the way: for example, when listening to a symphony, or watching a stunningly beautiful sunset, or staring for the first time into the eyes of your newborn child. The operations of the intellect are not welcome there. Deep down I have always known that these are the most important moments of my life.

The title of this chapter comes from the same-titled chapter of the book *Steps to an Ecology of Mind*, by the anthropologist Gregory Bateson, from which this basic idea arose.

SALKA

Salka is like a wind that blows through consensus reality from beyond, bringing us into contact with the great mystery and beauty of existence. (Oakley Gordon)

Salka is a Quechua word for natural or undomesticated energy. The wolf is salka while the dog is domesticated; the condor is salka while the chicken is domesticated; the deer is salka while the sheep is domesticated. It is not quite accurate to say that some beings are more salka than others. It might be better to say that some beings are more domesticated than others. Salka is the natural, free, energy of life and so all beings have salka. In domesticated beings, however, domestication is like a veneer through which the light of salka must shine.

We members of Western society have to be domesticated in order to survive in the environment that our society has created. What time we get up; how we dress; how we make a living; what we do for entertainment; what we eat and drink; the various roles we play as friend, spouse, child, parent, coworker, consumer, and citizen are all drawn from the list of options provided by our society. Even more important than the domestication of our time and energy, however, is the domestication of our concept of self, our understanding of who we are as Beings in this Cosmos. The very concept of who we are as Beings in this Cosmos may seem strange to consider as it takes us outside of our domesticated self and our role in our society and it touches instead upon our salka.

Being a domesticated human opens the door to all of the comforts and opportunities that our society can provide. There are, however, two major drawbacks to this domestication: one is that our society has created an environment where the default route to success involves engaging in actions that are killing our planet; the other is that our society only recognizes and reinforces part of the totality of who we are (our veneer). If I want to dance with life I need to be able to dance with my domesticated society, but I also want to dance with the vast mystery that is the Cosmos.

Salka is another part of our heritage as Beings in this Cosmos. We are alive, we exist, we are expressions of Nature and the Cosmos, our essence is salka. Salka is beyond definition, beyond comprehension, it is vastly mysterious. As we are, in our essence, salka, the same can be said of us. We are beyond definition, we are beyond comprehension, we are vastly more mysterious Beings than our society has led us to believe. To reach the full expression of being human we need to know both our salka and our domesticated selves. The Andean meditations get us in touch with salka.

AMÉRICO YÁBAR

My mentor, friend, and guide in the exploration of the Andean Cosmovision is the Peruvian mystic, don Américo Yábar. Don Américo serves as a *chakaruna*, a Quechua term for a human bridge connecting the energy of the Andes with that of the West. He is the founder of the Poetic Salka Movement on this planet. It is not a social movement or a political movement or a philosophical movement or a religious movement. It is a poetic movement. Expect a lot of love and beauty, joy and sadness, and no dogma. Américo once told me that poets suffer the beauty of the world. His goal is to help them connect with salka, then they will no longer suffer.

Américo Yábar (second from left) with paqos from the Qero region of Peru.

14

I first met don Américo in 1994. I went to several of his workshops in the United States and then began to travel to Peru to study with him there. When I have been in Peru he has also arranged for me to work with other paqos and healers of the Andes, and he has provided numerous opportunities for me to connect heart-to-heart  with the Andean people. There are some things I would like to share about Américo that reflect not only upon him but also upon the basic qualities of the path that he exemplifies, the path that attracted me, that I am sharing in this book.

I have been drawn to associate with Américo through his integrity, his love, and his joy of life. Walking your talk is for me a prerequisite for a path with a heart. Américo not only walks his talk, his walk is even more expressive and impressive than his talk (and as a mystic who is also a poet he talks very beautifully indeed). Everywhere I go with Américo in the Andes, from Cusco to the smallest village, people come running up with big smiles to greet him or lean out of windows to wave hello. In my most recent trip to Peru, we were driving down a remote dirt road when we passed a truck with a group of people in the back. A woman in the group spied Américo and with a big smile shouted out "Papa Américo! Papa Américo!" and waved at him as we drove by. Things like this happen all the time when I am with Américo.

The path Américo walks shows up profoundly in the way he interacts with the people of Peru, in his efforts to help them survive, and in his work to sustain the roots of their traditional culture. For all of that, Américo is not a saint nor a guru, he is just a

lovely human being. I find that attractive about this path as well—
as we travel it, we don't turn into Américo Yábar clones. Instead
we begin to blossom into our unique selves, and rather than rising above our humanity, we begin to express its true nature.

BASIC CONCEPTS

In this chapter I will begin to lay out the basic concepts of the Andean Cosmovision. These concepts don't define the Cosmovision, for it is not a set of beliefs. These concepts simply help you have the experiences that the Cosmovision makes possible, and it is those experiences that make up its heart. In our Western culture science and religion are defined by their concepts and beliefs. In the Andean Cosmovision the concepts and beliefs are like scaffolding that helps us build certain experiences; when that has been accomplished the scaffolding, the beliefs, can be discarded.

Here we go. Imagine that the Cosmos consists of a vast three-dimensional web of interconnected filaments of energy. Where these filaments of energy come together to form a bundle (a node) is what we experience as an object. I am a bundle of filaments in this vast network of filaments, as are you, as is the coffee mug sitting next to me as I type. Everything that exists is a node in this vast web of interconnected filaments; everything is connected to everything else. The Cosmos is thus one, unified whole (the vast web of filaments), and it is also a bunch of things (the bundles of filaments within the web).

Consciousness is viewed very differently in the Andean Cosmovision than it is in the West. We in the modern, Western world tend to equate our consciousness with our brain's ability to think. Because of this we assume that it takes a sophisticated nervous system, or at least some sort of nervous system, for consciousness to arise.

In the Andean Cosmovision, however, consciousness is seen as an inherent attribute of the filaments that make up the Cosmos. This means that everything is conscious since everything is made up of those filaments. I am conscious, you are conscious, my cat is conscious, the tree outside my window is conscious, the sun is conscious, the planet earth is conscious, the stones in the rivers are conscious.[1] The Cosmos as a whole is conscious (i.e., the Cosmic Consciousness). Rather than having a God who stands outside of creation, the Andeans see the Cosmos itself as a conscious Being with a creative impulse that organizes itself and changes over time.

Consciousness exists independently at all levels of the network of filaments that makes up the Cosmos. The various nodes within the Cosmos also have their own consciousness. The most important node in our neighborhood of the Cosmos is the *Pachamama*, the conscious entity who is our mother, the planet earth. She is not a transcendent spirit who lives in the planet earth, she is the conscious planet earth herself. She may be only part of the Cosmos but she has her own consciousness. The *Apus* are the great conscious Beings who are the majestic mountain peaks. While they are but part of the Pachamama, they have their own consciousness. And so on down the line. *Chakras* are the cultivated fields in the high Andes. They are daughters of the Pachamama, and while they are but part of the Pachamama, they have their own consciousness. When the villagers want to plant the field they consult with the chakra to see if this is the right time to plant and to honor and thank her for accepting the seeds.

Other important conscious Beings are *Tai Tai Inti* (the sun), *Mama Killa* (the moon), and *Mama Tuta* (the dark, the void, who holds the stars in her embrace). Then there are the stars themselves, and the trees, and the river that tumbles so beautifully down the side of the mountain. They are all conscious, and we can connect with them, and when we do our relationship with the rest of the Cosmos begins to blossom. This is the territory that the Andean Cosmovision opens up for us to explore.

— ENDNOTE —

[1] The following is Oakley the scientist speaking. The idea that stars, trees, and even stones are conscious is so far from how Western society views consciousness as to make the idea seem ludicrous to many people in our culture. From the perspective of the intellect, however, consciousness is and must remain the ultimate mystery of the universe, for consciousness, while it can be experienced, cannot be understood by thought. The intellect trying to understand consciousness is like a knife trying to cut its own edge. It is not a matter of not being clever enough, but rather a matter of logical impossibility. Consciousness exists beyond all of our concepts about it. Concepts and other things, such as direct experience, are the *contents* of consciousness, what we are aware of, not the part of us that is aware. Consciousness exists beyond all of our concepts of space and time and matter and energy and individual self (ego).

SALKA REVISITED

There are people who live in the high Andes who are very salka. You can see its light in their eyes, you can see the serenity in their faces, you can feel it inside yourself when they interact with you with warmth and shyness. Imagine being a young child living at 15,000 feet in the Andes. You live in your family's small stone house built of the material of the Pachamama. Such a house is known as a *wasi-tira* (literally a 'house of the earth'). The heart of the house is the *quncha*, an oven made of earth that forms a hardened hollow dome of adobe with an opening on the side for feeding wood into the fire and a few openings on top that are just the right size to sit the pots. You awake in the morning to the warmth of the quncha and the aroma of the soup that your mother is cooking for the family. Climbing out from under the llama skins you prepare to take your family's alpacas and llamas up the mountain to feed. You take along your *waraka*, a woven sling that you use to throw rocks to the side of the herd to direct them where you want them to go and to ward off the pumas, the condors, and the foxes of the high Andes.

As the frost disappears from the mountain's side in the first rays of the sun you slowly lead the herd up the mountain to 16,000 feet, where there is ichu grass upon which they can feed. You find a comfortable place to sit. A thousand feet below is your home, a little smoke coming out of the hole in the roof. Up here, however, all is wild. Despite your being at 16,000 feet the Andean peaks tower high above you. All you hear is the soft steps of the alpacas as they graze and the wind coming down from the mountains. The air is clear and the towering peaks, although they are miles away, seem almost close enough to touch. Below you a condor glides down the valley barely moving its wing tips to control its flight. You notice clouds gathering around the Apus, perhaps the Apus will send rain in your direction, or the deadly thunder and lightning. As you sit looking at the Apus you can feel that they are as aware of you as you are of them. This is salka, you are surrounded by salka, and you are salka, too.

In Peru I have gazed out over cultivated fields on the sides of mountains on slopes so steep that it is hard to stand. The fields have been cultivated for hundreds or even thousands of years. It is hard to put into words, but the farmland feels as wild as the national parks in the United States. It is as if the people who live there are as natural as the condors and the pumas and the wind that blows through the trees.

On one of my trips to Peru we traveled to a very salka village high in the Andes. To get there we had to drive for six hours on a dirt road from Cusco and then get on horses and travel for two days through the mountains, going over two 17,000-foot passes. The village itself was at 15,000 feet. We set up camp on the other side of a hill from the village. The next morning I got up and had a cup of coffee and sat on a stone watching the sun rise. I began to write in my journal. Looking up I was surprised to see a small girl staring at me from a few feet away. She was very salka, and she had come from the village to check us out. There began one of the most moving moments of my life, and at that moment my friend just happened to lean out of her tent and take our picture.

I didn't speak Quechua and she of course didn't speak English. But I have been the father of young children and I know how to communicate without the necessity that the words be

understood. I touched her necklace and told her how pretty it was and I said other nice things to her with an open heart. Then she settled down with me and we watched the day slowly begin to unfold, in complete salka together.

MAMA TUTA DANCED

In the beginning was Mama Tuta, the dark, the void. Then Mama Tuta began to dance, and as she danced the stars streamed out of her elbows, out of her knees, out of her breasts, out of her womb, and as she danced the stars were strewn across the universe.

MEDITATION: BELLYBUTTON TO THE PACHAMAMA

This is the first of many meditations I will be sharing in this book. The meditations are the heart of the Andean Cosmovision; they provide the path for actually exploring the new territory that the Cosmovision opens up for us. I call them meditations only because I can't come up with a better term. Sometimes I refer to them as meditative-like processes, which is a bit more accurate but is a rather awkward label. What they are in essence are ways of changing our experience of reality.

The meditations we will be looking at involve following some pretty unusual instructions, such as "connect your energy with the energy of the Pachamama." How do you go about actually doing something like that? The answer is you do it with *intent*. Now, intent is a pretty interesting thing, and we will be going further into its depths as the book progresses. To start off with, think of intent simply as sincere pretending. That is all it takes. You sincerely pretend to do the various steps of the meditations and see what happens.

This is a very simple meditation. It is the first meditation I learned from don Américo and he told us that if we were to do just this one meditation on a daily basis that it would have a profound effect on our lives. My ears perk up when I hear something like that.

First, I recommend for all of the meditations that you take a moment at the beginning to notice how you feel, to get a sense of what your energy feels like before you start. This will provide a baseline for you to determine how the meditation affects you.

Now here is how to do this meditation: Lie on the ground on your stomach and pull up your shirt far enough so that your bellybutton (navel) is in physical contact with the Pachamama (that great Cosmic Being who is our mother, the planet Earth).

If you have some energy you would like to get rid of (e.g., stress, anger, depression, sorrow, anxiety), then, using your intent (sincere pretending) let that energy flow from you and into the Pachamama through your bellybutton. Don't be concerned about giving this energy to her, it is not like pollution. The Pachamama takes this energy and recycles it into more refined energy that is then released into the Cosmos. This is one of her great gifts to us. If you would like, you can use your stomach muscles to press your bellybutton to the Pachamama with a few gentle pushes. This can help you guide your intent. Continue with this meditation until you feel that the undesirable energy has left your body.

In addition to, or instead of, sending the Pachamama the energy you would like to get rid of, you can ask her to give you some energy that you could use (e.g., tranquility, love, ease, harmony, groundedness). Using your intent (sincere pretending) ask her for the energy you need and let that energy flow up from the Pachamama through your bellybutton and into your Being. This can be facilitated by gently drawing in your stomach muscles a few times as if pulling her energy into you. Continue until you feel complete.

When you are finished with the meditation, take a few moments to notice how you feel, to get in touch with what your energy is like after the meditation. The difference between how you felt before the meditation and how you feel after is the only meaning of the meditation. Sincere pretending is all it takes to get an effect, and the effect is what matters. If the shift in your energy is in a direction that seems good to you, then consider continuing to explore this meditation in the future.

This meditation is very simple but the effects (particularly when repeated over several days) can be quite beautiful. Connecting our energy with Nature and the Cosmos is what the Andean meditations are all about. They enhance our *salka*, our natural, undomesticated energy.

The Andean meditations are the outward form of something deeper, a shift in our relationship with Nature and the Cosmos. It is from this relationship that the effects of the Andean meditations arise, and the organizing principle of this relationship is *ayni*.

Ayni is the Andean principle of reciprocity, a balance of giving and receiving that reflects the underlying dynamics of the Cosmos. As you engage in this meditation with the Pachamama, I can't imagine that a deep sense of love and gratitude for the Pachamama won't arise. To follow the Andean path, nourish this relationship with the Pachamama, create balance in the relationship, give something in love to her in return. Quite simply express to her your heart-felt gratitude for what she gives you in this meditation. Often, as a simple form of ayni, I pour a few drops of wine or tequila onto the Pachamama in gratitude and with the intent that it honor her and nourish her. In this way I am sending energy back to her in reciprocity. This offering is not a bribe or a payment for services rendered. It is instead like giving flowers unbidden to a loved one. We will be covering more formal and elaborate offerings (called despachos) and taking a deeper look at ayni in later chapters.

INTENT

In our first meditation I introduced *intent*, as it is used in the context of this book, as sincere pretending. The way you carry out the various steps in the Andean meditations is simply by sincerely pretending that you are doing so. That is all it takes to get an effect from a meditation and so that is all the understanding of intent you need to explore the vast experiential realm available through the Andean Cosmovision. At that level, intent is easy to understand, but as we go deeper into what intent really is, it becomes more and more mysterious.

Let us consider both parts of sincere pretending. First note that it involves pretending, which takes us outside the realm of having to distinguish between True and False to a place where we don't have to be either skeptical or gullible, because we are just pretending. Second, for intent to work the pretending needs to be sincere. Sincerity is an interesting thing. What does it mean to be sincere? Why is it that it doesn't make sense to ask whether or not a computer is being sincere, while it does make sense to ask whether or not a person is being sincere? The answer, I believe, is that sincerity involves something more than thought. Sincerity has to do with the heart, and through the heart with something deeper where words cannot penetrate. Despite that cryptic comment, I'll have some more words to say about intent as we progress through this book.

THE MASK

Joseph Campbell, the great comparative mythologist, wrote a book about the role of masks in ancient ceremonies (*The Masks of God: Primitive Mythology*). He was interested in the experiences of people who participated in sacred rituals where a performer wore a mask that portrayed her or him as a deity. The people at the ceremony usually knew the identity of the person wearing the mask. It may have been, for example, an uncle of theirs, so what did they believe about the person when he was wearing the mask in the ceremony? Did they believe that in the ceremony the mask actually transformed him into the deity or did they see him as representing the deity in a metaphorical sort of way?

Campbell argues that the people at these ceremonies did not take either perspective. Those who believe that the mask transforms the person into a deity, the *true believers*—and this would include anyone who believes that their religion is literally true—do not belong at the ceremony. On the other hand, the spoilsports, the *skeptics* for whom the mask has no power to transform its wearer into a deity, for whom the ritual must at best represent a metaphorical transformation, are also not invited. According to Campbell, the statues of guardians—warriors, dragons, demons—who flank the entranceways into the ancient ceremonial sites are there to keep out what today we might call the religious mind as well as the scientific mind. The people at these ancient ceremonies took a third option, experiencing the ritual as neither literally true nor essentially metaphorical, immersing themselves instead in the realm of what Campbell calls 'as if'. The realm of 'as if' sounds an awful lot to me like the realm of intent.

The anthropologist Gregory Bateson had something similar to say:

> "[In the 1500s] in Europe, many Catholics and Protestants were burning each other at the stake, or were willing to be burned, rather than compromise about the nature of the bread and wine used in the Mass. The Catholics said that the bread *is* the body of Christ and the wine *is* the blood, the Protestants said, on the other hand, that the bread *stands for* the body of Christ and the wine *stands for* the blood. The point is not to say that one side is better than the other, but that the argument is one of fundamental importance in understanding the nature of the sacred and human nature ... Now it is my suspicion that the richest use of the word 'sacred' is that use which will say that what matters is the combination of the two, getting the two together. And that any fracturing of the two is anti-sacred. The Catholics and the Protestants were equally anti-sacred. The bread both is and stands for the body." (*A Sacred Unity: Further Steps to an Ecology of Mind*)

Bateson goes on to say that the path to the sacred involves leaving what he labels 'prose thinking' (and that I label as 'the intellect') and entering into 'dream thinking,' for in dreams our experiences are not labelled as true or false, or as literally true or as metaphorical. They simply are.

Photo of the Dan mask courtesy of the ArtyFactory: www.artyfactory.com/

MEDITATION: TOUCHING PACHAMAMA

This is a very simple meditation (like the Bellybutton to the Pachamama meditation). After years and years of seeking to know more and more, I find that I have returned to the simple meditations as the foundation for integrating the Andean Cosmovision into my life.

This meditation is very useful for coming into harmony and balance within ourselves. I don't use this meditation to get rid of unwanted energy (e.g. anger, anxiety, stress)—there are other processes for that—I use it when I have become too focussed on only part of who I am. For me this often means that I have gotten way too much into my head, thinking about the world (and often worrying about it) rather than experiencing it. This meditation is also beneficial for recovering from other ways we might be imbalanced, for example, when we are too caught up in our emotions, or when we are feeling spacey or ungrounded. One thing I particularly like about this meditation is that it helps me get in touch with *all* of who I am, not just part of me.

In this meditation we bring the various aspects of our Being into harmony with each other by bringing them into harmony with the energy of the Pachamama. Being in harmony with the energy of the Cosmos, in this case the Pachamama, is a large part of what the Andean Cosmovision is all about. When we are in harmony with the Pachamama our sense of self expands, and we find it easier to surf the rough waters we sometimes find in our lives.

Here is the meditation in all of its simplicity. Sit on the ground. Begin by noticing the state of your energy, i.e., notice how it feels to be you right now. Take a few seconds to do this. Now place your hands on the Pachamama (our mother Earth) and with *intent* (sincere pretending) connect the energy of your body through you hands with the energy of the Pachamama. Ask her to bring your energy into harmony with hers. With intent, connect the various aspects of your Being one at a time with the Pachamama: your physical body (focus on the area just below your belly button), your emotions (focus on your heart), and your intellect (focus on the crown of your head). Notice how your energy in that area shifts as you connect to the Pachamam. Continue until you feel the shift is complete. Sincerely thank the Pachamama. Spend a few seconds being aware of your new state of energy, how you feel being you. That's it.

This meditation takes only a few minutes, but if you do it on a daily basis (combined with simple acts of *ayni*), it will have a very nice effect on your life.

I often use this Touching Pachamama meditation to prepare my energy for other meditations I am about to do. In fact, I almost always start off my meditations with the Touching Pachamama meditation. I want to add, however, the idea that nothing should be done *all* the time. A meditation that is done *all* the time faces the risk of turning into an intent-less ritual. Let each time you sit yourself down (or stand yourself up) to meditate be a time of spontaneity. Check out your energy and what is going on in your life and select a meditation or meditations that feel right for the moment. We are in a dance,with ourselves, with each other, with the Pachamama, with the Cosmos. Find joy in the dance. Be light on your feet.

HUCHA

There are many Andean meditations for getting rid of *hucha* (pronounced 'hoocha'). Hucha is translated as heavy or discordant or chaotic energy. For me the prototypical example of hucha is how I feel after a bad day at work. My energy feels heavy and unpleasant and I feel disconnected from the underlying beauty of the world. Note that hucha is not evil or negative energy; the Andean Cosmovision just doesn't look at the world in that way. Hucha is not accompanied by a moral evaluation and there is no moral imperative to get rid of hucha, in yourself or in others. Getting rid of hucha simply moves us from an unpleasant state to a much more pleasant one.

Our hucha is also hard on those around us. Back when I was a full-time professor I would sometimes come home full of hucha. Even though I would try to keep it to myself, it would still spread from me to my family; after a few minutes my wife would stop being as happy and even my sons in the next room would start to bicker with each other. In contexts where we are intimately connected with another person (e.g., in a therapy or a healing setting) hucha seems to spread very easily. In the Andes there are many, many ways of getting rid of hucha in yourself and in others. We will take a look at several ways of getting rid of hucha in this book.

I like to get rid of my hucha before I engage in other meditations. It is a great way to prepare my energy before venturing through the door into the Andean Cosmovision. I often do the

Touching the Pachamama meditation (covered in the previous chapter) followed by the Releasing Hucha meditation (introduced in the next chapter) before I move on to other Andean meditations.

If I may wax theoretical for a moment, hucha arises when our society or our ego places demands upon us that take us out of harmony with our natural state of being. Society has created a world where for us to live and succeed we need to follow rules that are often disconnected from our relationship with Nature. Our society, however, is what it is and unless we want to become hermits we need to operate within it. Operating within our society almost inevitably leads to hucha, but we can release it, leaving us free to be in harmony with the essence of who we are and with the larger systems of Nature and the Cosmos. When we get rid of our hucha we not only feel better, we bring beauty to our dance with our society, and that has a nice effect on those around us as well.

MEDITATION:
RELEASING HUCHA

This simple meditation is my favorite way of getting rid of my own hucha. It feels good (I'm not sure 'good' quite encompasses it) and it provides a doorway through which to explore experientially the Andean Cosmovision. Getting rid of hucha is also a preliminary step for other Andean meditations. This is particularly important to do before working with other people (so you don't give them your hucha) or after working with others (in case you picked up their hucha). This meditation is derived from a meditation in Joan Wilcox's excellent book, Masters of the Living Energy: The Mystical World of the Q'ero of Peru (see the recommended reading section at the end of the book for the complete reference). Here is how to do it.

Sit on the ground[1], it is ok to sit on a blanket or a sitting pad. Sit comfortably upright with your spine oriented vertically (because that is the direction the energy is going to flow).

First, notice how your energy feels, what it feels like to be you right now. If you would like, begin with the Touching the Pachamama meditation.

Then, with intent (sincere pretending) open up your energy field at the bottom of your spine and let your hucha begin to flow down into the Pachamama. Don't be concerned about giving the Pachamama your hucha, it is not like polluting her,. The Pachamama accepts our hucha and recycles it into refined energy, releasing it back into the Cosmo. It is one of her great gifts to us.

Right after you open up your energy field at the bottom of your spine, use intent again to open up your energy field at the top of your head and invite the light, refined energy of the Cosmos to flow down into your Being to replace the hucha that is flowing into the Pachamama.

Feel the hucha leaving your body and the refined energy of the Cosmos flowing in to take its place. Continue until you sense that all the hucha has been released. If there are places where the hucha seems stuck just be patient, keep up your intent of releasing the hucha. I sometimes ask the Pachamama to spiral her energy up into that spot to gently wash the hucha away.

When all of your hucha has left, thank the Pachamama and the Cosmos. Then, notice how you feel.

The difference between how you felt when you started and how you feel when you have completed the meditation comprises your knowledge of what the meditation has accomplished. Any description you read about what a meditation accomplishes is completely irrelevant. What a meditation actually accomplishes for you is whatever it accomplishes for you. The effects may not be the same each time, and they may vary from very subtle to wow, but over several times you will begin to learn what the meditation is all about. This won't be an intellectual knowledge (or you *could* just read about it) but instead will be knowledge at a deeper level of your Being. This is what the exploration of the Andean Cosmovision is all about: an exploration that takes place in a something-other-than-intellectual level.

As with all the Andean meditations, this meditation is performed within the context of our relationship with the Cosmos. The Pachamama accepts and recycles our hucha, the Cosmos gives us refined and beautiful energy to replace it. It is a wonderful reality we live in where the Earth, the wind, the trees, the rivers, the stars, the mountain peaks, the Cosmos itself are willing to support our evolution as Beings. This all happens within a loving and mutually supportive relationship between ourselves and the Cosmos. The most essential element of this relationship, again, is the Andean principle of *ayni* (reciprocity) where to receive is always balanced by giving in return and to give is always balanced by receiving in return.

Ayni is not an intellectual or ethical concept, but rather something that arises from the heart. After wandering down the path of the Andean Cosmovision for a while, a great sense of gratitude and love for the living Cosmos arose within me. I always bring a little plastic bottle of tequila (it doesn't have to be tequila) and offer a little to the Pachamama and to the Apus (the Beings who are the great mountain peaks) and to the river by which I meditate and to the trees and to the stars. Occasionally I will offer a more formal expression of gratitude, a *despacho*, which I will describe in a later chapter.

— ENDNOTE —

[1] I prefer to do this meditation while sitting on the ground. After you have become familiar with the meditation and its effects you can do it while sitting in a chair in an upper floor of a high-rise hotel. I really prefer, however, to do this meditation in the intimacy of actual physical contact with the Pachamama. The effect is juicier, and that is particularly important when first learning the meditation so that you can get a better idea of what it has to offer.

AYNI

Ayni is such a fundamental aspect of the Andean Cosmovision that I would like to pause and describe it in more detail. The essence of ayni is reciprocity, that is, when you receive something you give something in return, and when you give something you receive something in return. This keeps balance in the relationship, but it also does more than that. It nourishes the relationship as well. It is really quite unlike giving money in exchange for something at the store. It is not a matter of breaking even in an exchange. It is like a spiral where the cycle of giving and receiving elevates both parties and continues to elevate as the cycle is repeated.

Ayni informs the Andean people's relationships with each other, and in that context it can be easily understood. It is when the Andean people apply ayni to their relationship with Nature and the Cosmos that we move into mysterious territory and begin to glimpse the profound beauty of their Cosmovision. To understand how ayni works in this context we first need to understand their very different view of Nature and the Cosmos. It is not possible to have a true relationship with inert, mindless, matter. In the Western view of reality that is how rivers and stones and trees and the Cosmos itself are basically seen. Within our Western worldview we can love a forest or the Earth, but it is hard to conceive of them loving us back. The Andean people have a very different experience of reality, one that allows a true, not just metaphorical, relationship between humans and Nature and the Cosmos.

Let us begin by looking at ayni in the context of the Andean people and their relationships with each other. Ayni shows up

Villagers threshing wheat.

clearly in the work that the people in a village perform together. When it is time to work a family's field, the men and women in the community unite to work it as a community. The sowing of a field, for example, involves a line of men working foot plows to overturn the soil, followed by a line of women who plant the seeds (these relative roles of the sexes reflect other aspects of the Cosmovision that I will cover later). When such communal work is done the recipients rarely express thanks, for it is just part of life that they will then establish balance by working their neighbors' fields in turn. When you give you receive, and when you receive you give. Balance is maintained, both sides are nourished, and the community is healthy.

> *Reciprocity is like a pump at the heart of Andean life. The constant give-and-take of ayni...maintains a flow of energy throughout the ayllu [community].* (Allen, 2002, pg 73).*

---

*   All references can be found in the Recommended Reading section at the end of this book.

I would like to share some of my own experiences with ayni from the perspective of a Westerner entering into a relationship with the Andean people. My trips to Peru involve working with various paqos and healers, and this "working with" often involves my participation in the ceremonies and healing rituals that they provide. What I can give them in return to balance our relationship, what they really need that I have, is money.

At the beginning of my exploration of the Andean Cosmovision I felt uncomfortable giving money in reciprocity. From my Western perspective it just didn't seem right to give money in exchange for a sacred experience. There is a lot of cultural background to my feelings. Our culture has some strong views about the relationship between the sacred and the secular, and how when the two are mixed in the wrong way then what should be sacred becomes profane instead. What comes to my mind as examples are the practice of religions selling forgiveness and tel-evangelists getting rich by asking people to show their love for God by sending them money.

While ayni can take the form of money, however, ayni is not the same thing as payment. Ayni brings people closer together. The goal is balance rather than gain, mutual support rather than advantage. When I was able to shift from my culture's worldview to the Andean Cosmovision, I was able to enter into the true ayni of the relationship I was nourishing with the Andean paqos and healers. On their side they were willing to do the same, to inter-act with me in ayni within the context of the ceremony, rather than slipping into the Western, capitalistic relationship that is encroaching into their culture. When the ceremony is over and ayni has been completed by my giving them money, then the context usually does shift. The sense of the sacred evaporates as they pull out their goods for sale, and some hard haggling begins. The two ways of being in relationship, one of ayni within the context of the sacred and one of sales within the context of commerce, could not be more different.

I would like to share another example of how ayni works in Peru. This specific instance occurred in one of my more recent trips. I had brought along some extra money to give to the people of Peru, not much, but it doesn't take much to help someone who lives in the high Andes. The challenge was to find a context in which I could give the money as ayni, rather than as charity from a (comparatively) rich Westerner to needy indigenous people (which is not ayni at all).

Don Américo helped me with this. He is a genius at shaping my well-intentioned efforts into something more beautiful than I anticipated. In this case we were in a very small village high in the Andes, this location was probably important to our success as there the people still lived a life governed by ayni.

I was introduced to several people whom Américo knew could use some help. First, I was introduced to a middle-aged man who was suffering from severe diarrhea. He asked if I had anything to help. Being the well-prepared westerner that I am, of course I had medication for diarrhea. I gave him some with instructions on how to take it. He thanked me most sincerely, and a few minutes later he returned to give me three eggs from his hens, which I thought was pretty nice of him. Then I was introduced to two young girls who were orphans and needed some money to get school supplies (in the small villages there are few resources for people who live outside any family). They were friendly but shy. I gave them some money, and with big smiles they each gave me a hug. Then one ran out and returned with a belt she had made and gave it to me as a present. The village Club of Mothers (who meet weekly to pursue activities for the benefit of the children in the village) gave me a live chicken in ayni for my financial support. And at the end of the day I was introduced to a very old woman (more than 100 years old) whose family were all gone, and I gave her the rest of what I had. She grasped my hand with both of hers and looked into my eyes with a gentle smile and said something to me in Quechua, which

Américo then translated for me. She said that she had nothing she could give me, so she would pray for me that night in her dreams. I couldn't imagine getting anything nicer than that.

Ayni in the relationships among humans may be reasonably easy for us to understand from our own cultural perspective, but when we look at the Andean people's ayni with the animals upon which they depend, then we start to move into new territory. I would like to talk about the relationship between the Andean people and their traditional domesticated animals, specifically alpacas and llamas. The following description pertains to people who live in isolated villages in the high Andes and who still live the Andean Cosmovision. These people and their animals and their plants, barely eke out a living at altitudes as high as 15,000 feet in villages that may be a two-day walk from the nearest road.

The alpacas and llamas make it possible for the Andean people to live at such altitudes. Unlike other ruminants, alpacas and llamas can graze upon the sparse, high-altitude grass without damaging it. Llamas carry loads to and from the fields and from one village to another. They can carry 70- to 90-pound packs up to 16 miles a day. The hides and wool from both llamas and alpacas are used for clothing. Wool from the alpacas is sold in market towns to obtain sugar and flour and other materials that cannot be produced in the village. Dung from the animals fertilizes the high-altitude fields or when dried can be used as fuel. It is not a very hot fuel. One time we decided to make hot chocolate at 17,000 feet over a fire of alpaca dung and it took an hour for the water to get slightly warm.

The Andean people recognize that their alpacas and llamas cannot survive without human protection, and they recognize equally that humans cannot survive without the alpacas and llamas. The people and their animals share the same resources and the same weather and the same hardships of life at high altitudes, and they also share the same festivals. The llamas and alpacas are not seen as resources to be managed, rather they are seen as partners in a mutually supportive dance of reciprocity among Beings.

The llamas and alpacas are treated with love and respect. An Andean herder knows every llama and alpaca by sight and by name. The llamas and alpacas participate—adorned—in sacred ceremonies, so that the ceremonies may make them happy too. They join the people in appealing to Nature and the Cosmos in times of need. Special ceremonies are held in honor of the llamas and alpacas. In the llama ch'allay ceremony, for example, the llamas are given chicha (locally brewed corn beer) to thank them for all their work in carrying the harvests up the mountain. During the ceremony a small bell is rung near the llama's ear to clean its energy.

When an alpaca or llama is sacrificed or killed for food, the event calls for a special ritual. The animal's feet are tied together, and it is laid upon the ground with its head in a person's lap. The person sings to the animal and strokes its head and gently feeds it coca leaves. At the appropriate moment the animal is killed swiftly. As it dies its feet are untied so that its spirit may begin its run to the sacred mountain, Apu Asungate, accompanied by prayers that Asungate may receive the spirit and send it back to be born again in the same corral. Through its death the animal's spirit is a gift to the Apu, who returns the spirit back to the herd in ayni.

> *As the life force [of the animal] flows towards the mountains and back in perfect reciprocity, the cosmic balance is maintained.* (Bolin, 1998, pg 56).

Now we will take a step yet further away from the Western view of reality to consider ayni in the relationship of humans with the Cosmos. The Pachamama (the great mother who is the planet Earth) is but a part of the conscious Cosmos, yet she has her own consciousness, and the chakras (fields in which crops are grown) are daughters of the Pachamama and have their own consciousness as well. Each chakra is responsible for the crop that is grown upon her, and each chakra has a name given by the people who work that field. Before entering a chakra to work the people give a brief ritual of gratitude and respect to the Pachamama and her daughter. A little chicha (corn beer) may be poured upon the ground to slake their thirsts. Upon leaving the field another brief ritual may given to thank them for their generosity, and in this way ayni is nourished. At that time a little thanks may also be given to Illapa, the god of thunder, thanking him for sending the rain (and for not sending lightning).

On one of my trips to Peru we stopped to watch the people gather a harvest of potatoes. It was in the high Andes on the land between Cusco and the Sacred Valley. The numerous plots were all small and at different stages of ripeness and contained various crops. The ground stretching up to the mountains looked like a patchwork quilt upon the lap of the Pachamama. Thin trails of smoke rose from a dozen small fires scattered across the land. The fires were tended by young mothers and old women. The first potatoes taken out of the ground in the morning had been placed back into holes dug in the Pachamama, covered with earth, and then a fire was lit above them, cooking the potatoes for a meal later in the day. The custom is both practical and sacred, honoring the Pachamama, nourishing her children, and maintaining the relationship between the Earth and those who live off her bounty.

After appreciating this sight, we piled back into our van to continue on our way. As we pulled out, my gaze fell upon a young woman tending a fire near the road perhaps 20 yards away. She looked to be in her early twenties. She was wearing the traditional full skirt and wool sweater of the Andes made of a woven fabric dyed in colorful shades of green and brown, and she sported a tan hat with a rounded top and a wide flat brim. She was sitting on the ground, in intimate contact with the Pachamama,

nursing her child. As the van pulled away she looked up and for a moment our eyes met, and she smiled. It was the most beautiful smile I have ever seen, a smile that conveyed an absolute contentment with life-at-that-moment, a smile from the heart of the Pachamama.

In the Andean Cosmovision humans are not distinct from Nature nor is Nature distinct from the Cosmos. The role of humans is not to use Nature for our own good nor to serve as stewards over it but instead to interact with Nature in a dance of respect and mutual support. We are but part of the fabric of life, not its apex; we are children of the Pachamama, but not her special children.

In the Andes ayni goes beyond the people's relationships with each other and with animals and with fields to inform their relationships with the Cosmos. When the Andeans gather together socially or in ceremony or to do communal work, they perform brief ceremonies to invite into their circle the Pachamama and the Apus and other great Beings of the Cosmos, to honor them and to express respect and gratitude. This is all done as ayni, to nourish a relationship of mutual support and service. They serve the Cosmos and the Cosmos serves them, and from this their sense of relationship becomes stronger. Ayni is not tit for tat, but rather it nourishes the relationship, making it stronger and deeper.

Ayni is the pump that keeps the energy flowing through the people and their Cosmos. The importance of ayni, however, is sometimes lost when the Andean Cosmovision is translated into the Western world view. Some people in the West view the Cosmovision primarily as a technology for personal transformation. This is understandable as our culture is much more into technology than it is into relationships. It also fits the Western mind set that Nature is to be harnessed, controlled, used for our benefit. When viewed that way the importance of completing the circle of ayni with Nature can be overlooked. The meditations, however, are *fundamentally* about nourishing a loving and mutually supportive *relationship* with Nature and the Cosmos. The benefits of the meditations *come from this relationship*, and to not attend to that is to miss the truly revolutionary and beautiful aspects of what can emerge from the Andean Cosmovision. I apologize for using italics to *stress the things I really care about*, I can get a bit carried away at times.

This chapter on ayni draws heavily from the work (which I quoted and paraphrased) of the anthropologist Inge Bolin in her beautiful book *Rituals of Respect: The Secret of Survival in the High Peruvian Andes*. I would also like to thank Monique Duphily whose dissertation on the topic of ayni contributed to the writing of this chapter.

MEDITATION: LOVE TO PACHAMAMA

Here is a little meditation that I like to use in my introductory presentations to give people who have never experienced the Andean Cosmovision a taste of what it is all about. First I talk about the Pachamama and then I introduce intent as sincere pretending and then I talk them through this meditation. You can do this meditation while sitting (in a chair is fine) or standing, but usually my audience is sitting in chairs.

To begin, uncross your legs and arms and sit comfortably erect (so that your spine forms a good conduit to the flow of energy from the Cosmos to the Pachamama). You may find it helpful to close your eyes while doing this. Pay attention to a few breaths just to get your mind out of your thoughts and into your experience as a living Being.

Using your intent (sincere pretending), open the energy field at the top of your head and let the light, refined, energy of the Cosmos flow down through the top of your head and into your heart. Pause to experience this.

As you experience this flow of energy into your heart, let your heart transform that energy into love. Then, let this love flow down your spine and into the Pachamama, sending that love to her.

Spend a while just experiencing the energy flowing down through your head and into your heart, there being transformed into love, and then that love flowing into the Pachamama. You may notice, after a while, the Pachamama sending love back up into you to your heart.

That's it. Opening up to the flow of energy, transforming it (into love), sending it on (to the Pachamama—these are basic processes of being a paqo.

This meditation is a nice way to get a taste of the Andean Cosmovision. If you like the taste then you might want to keep exploring. There is also more to it, in addition to the nice effect it may have on us. This meditation starts to change our relationship with the natural world and with the Cosmos. When relationships change then the relata (the things that are in the relationship....we ourselves, the Pachamama, the Cosmos) begin to change as well. This is setting the context for things to begin to blossom further down the line.

THE THREE CENTERS
OF BEING

The Andean Cosmovision views each of us as being a bundle or node in the network of energetic filaments that constitute the Cosmos. While each of us is a whole Being—not a collection of isolated parts—there are areas or neighborhoods within us that have their own special quality of energy. There are many overlapping ways in which we can identify complementary aspects of ourselves. The Cosmovision, for example, draws a distinction between the energy on the right side and left side of our body, and between aspects of ourselves that are tied to the past, the present, and the future. We will be looking at those various aspects as we work through this book. In this chapter we will take a look at three centers of our Being that each has its own way of perceiving and understanding reality. In Quechua they are called the *llankay*, the *munay*, and the *yachay*.

The llankay organizes the energy of our physical body. It is located a couple of finger-breadths below our navel and a few inches inside the body. The Quechua word llankay is sometimes translated into English as work. It is through our llankay that we can bring our body to bear to change the physical world around us. At the very center of the llankay, however, is an infinitesimal point of not-being, where we are "no-thing". That is rather esoteric so don't worry about it. The important concept is that the llankay is the energetic center of our physical Being.

The munay is located in the area of our heart and is the center of love. The love associated with the munay, however, is not an emotion. Emotions are tightly connected to our thoughts, for how we respond emotionally to an event is largely a result of how we think about it. The love in the munay has nothing to do with romance or sex or sentimentality or jealousy. Through our munay we can experience our connection with the rest of the Cosmos. The filaments of the Cosmos have an underlying frequency, and we can feel that frequency in our munay (for we are made of those same filaments). This beautiful and ineffable experience of the underlying energetic frequency of the Cosmos gets labeled with the closest available term, which in English is love. There is a whole universe to explore through the munay. The paqos of the Andes are as knowledgeable and skilled at working with the munay as Western scientists are at building computers and spaceships.

The yachay is the energy center located in the crown of the head. It is the seat of our intellect, and it is from the yachay that our thoughts emerge. In the West we associate consciousness only with the yachay and we usually experience our consciousness as being located somewhere behind our eyeballs. It is possible, however, to move our consciousness to the munay or to the llankay and experience reality in a very different way. This is part of the exploration of the totality of who we are that the Andean Cosmovision makes possible. We will see how to go about exploring our three centers in upcoming meditations.

All three of these centers comprehend the world around us and organize our responses, and they do so in fundamentally different ways that are completely incomprehensible to each other. The yachay (intellect), for example, will never understand the munay or the llankay. The munay cannot understand the yachay or llankay, and so on. We are not, however, just a set of three separate ways of understanding the world. The yachay, munay, and llankay are three facets of who we are, but we are the diamond that has those facets.

My experiences in Peru, and meditating back here in the United States, have led me into my munay. My intellect (my yachay) cannot truly understand those experiences. This has been a challenge for me. I grew up as a boy-scientist and my career has been in academia (which is about as yachay as you can get). It was more than a little hard for my intellect to accept that it could not understand my munay experiences and that it never would. Something eventually happened, however, which I will try to express in words. There is a part of us that is beyond or deeper than our three energy centers, and in this part our three centers are simply different windows through which to view the world. It is at this deeper level that my munay, after years of hard work, confusion, pain, and joy has established its credibility. My yachay has the grace to acknowledge that the deeper part of me appreciates and values my explorations of munay, even if my yachay cannot understand it.

FOR A FUTURE OF BEAUTY
TO BE POSSIBLE

Metaphorically speaking Europe represents the yachay, the ability to think. With all due respect to my own society in the United States, there have been relatively few great philosophers from here. The United States, on the other hand, has a great penchant for technology; it represents the llankay, the ability to change the physical world. The people of the Andes—and I suspect the same is true for many of the indigenous cultures on this planet—represent the munay, the ability to directly experience our connection with Nature and the Cosmos.

I began this book by pointing out that we in modern society have all the technology and knowledge we need to turn this planet into a garden of Eden. We apparently lack the heart to do so. As a species we need to bring together and integrate our ability to think, our technology, and a direct experience of our connection with Nature: the yachay, the llankay, and the munay. I don't know how to do that at a societal level; maybe others will be able to figure it out. I do know how to do it a personal level; that is what I have been working on for years and is what I want to share in this book. Perhaps if enough people learn how to integrate their yachay, munay and llankay that change will inform our society

FATE OF THE MACHUKUNA

There are many stories woven into the fabric of the Andean culture. These stories differ from village to village and from storyteller to storyteller. The criterion I use to select which version to share with others is a very nonacademic one. I simply pick the one I like the most, which is usually the version that best guides me in my exploration of the Andean Cosmovision.

The indigenous people of the Andes refer to themselves as the *Runakuna*. In Quechua the word *runa* means person, and the addition of *kuna* to a word makes the word plural, so Runakuna simply translates as people. In its narrowest use, Runakuna refers to those Andeans who are the inheritors of, and who still live, the Andean Cosmovision. In its widest use Runakuna refers to the entire human race.

We are living in the age of the Runakuna, which is the age of the sun, and we are the children of the sun. Before there was the sun (Tay Tay Inti), there was the moon (Mama Killa), and before the Runakuna there were the Machukuna, the children of the moon, the Ancient Ones (Machu is Quechua for ancient). The Machukuna lived on this Earth and the moon was their sun.

The age of the Machukuna ended with a *pachakuti*. A pachakuti is a time when space, time, and consciousness go through a great change, an overturning of the way things were into a new way of being. In this pachakuti, the creative impulse of the living Cosmos created the sun, under whose searing light the Machukuna—the children of the moon—could not survive.

The Machukuna could see their doom approaching with the coming of the first dawn. Some fled into the hills to seek shelter in caves, some dove into deep waters, others hid in the trees. They all died, the sun killed them all, but their spirits are still around. Their spirits may be encountered in certain caves; and at night, in a bright moon, their bones are reanimated and they walk about the earth, tending the same fields at night that the Runakuna tend during the day. The *chullpas* (small stone dwellings built by the Machukuna) are scattered about the slopes of the Andes to this day. At sunset the Machukuna emerge from their chullpas and warm their bones by the red glow of the evening sky.[1]

Chullpas in the Andes.

With the rising of the sun and the fall of the Machukuna the Runakuna appeared and the age of the children of the sun began. Why did the creative impulse of the Cosmos create the sun and destroy the Machukuna? Some Andeans believe it was done to make way for us, the Runakuna, but others believe the Cosmos did it simply because it felt like it.

There have been other pachakutis in the history of this world and there will be more in the future. When a pachakuti occurs, the people must fundamentally change in the face of its new challenges or experience dire consequences. Many paqos in Peru believe that we are in a pachakuti right now. They believe that they have a piece of the solution for how we must change as a species. That is the reason the paqos have—after centuries of purposeful isolation from Western culture—opened up to the West to share with us what they know.

In my academic research on this topic I ran across the following. Fifty years ago an anthropologist talked with an Andean paqo about the pachacutis. He asked the paqo when the next pachacuti might occur. The paqo told him not to worry, that the next pachacuti would not arrive until the glaciers left the slopes of Apu Asungate.

— END NOTE —

[1] To say that the spirits of the Machukuna still live in our world/age/time may be too Western of a way of putting it. In the Andean view of time/place/consciousness, when there is a pachacuti, an upheaval in the world, the old world/age/time continues to exist but in a timeline that is parallel to our own, less real to us but still able to affect our world.

MEDITATION: TUNING THE THREE CENTERS OF BEING

This is a very beneficial meditation to do on a regular basis.

For this meditation, it helps to sit on the ground so that you can comfortably place your hands directly on the Pachamama. I usually begin by doing the Touching the Pachamama meditation followed by the Releasing Hucha meditation (these take only a couple of minutes and they do a good job of preparing our energy for this meditation).

First, notice what your energy feels like before you start. How does it feel to be you right now? This is the baseline from which you can evaluate the effect of this meditation.

Begin the meditation by placing either one of your hands on the Pachamama and the other on your body over your llankay (the center of your physical Being, located a couple of finger-breadths below your navel). With intent (sincere pretending), form an energetic connection through your hands between your llankay and the Pachamama, and ask the Pachamama to bring your llankay into harmony with her. Spend a while noticing the effect of this connection. Continue until you feel that the energy of your llankay is in harmony with the Pachamama (perhaps a couple of minutes).

Next, take your hand from your llankay and place it on the Pachamama and take the hand that was on the Pachamama and place it over your munay (your heart, the center of love where you can experience your connection with the Cosmos). With

56

intent, connect the energy of your munay with the Pachamama and ask her to bring your munay into harmony with her. Notice how the energy of your munay is different from the energy of your llankay.

When you sense that harmony with the Pachamama has been reached take your hand from your munay and place it on the Pachamama and put the hand that was on the Pachamama on your yachay (the center of thought, located at the crown of your head). Connect the energy of your yachay with the Pachamama, ask her to bring your yachay into harmony with her, and continue until you feel this process has been completed. Notice how the energy of your yachay is different from the energy of your munay and llankay.

Now follow the same steps again, but this time connect each of your centers one at a time with the refined energy of the Cosmos. Start by putting one hand over your llankay and raise the other hand toward the sky to connect with the energy of the Cosmos. With intent, open a connection between the two and ask the Cosmos to bring your llankay into harmony with it. Then bring your hand down from the Cosmos and put it over your munay and raise your other hand to the Cosmos. Finally, bring your hand down from the Cosmos and put it over your yachay and raise your other hand.

When you have finished notice your energy and how it feels to be you right now. How your energy shifts from before the meditation to after the meditation is the only meaning of the meditation. This can't be described, it can only be experienced. I recommend that you do this on a regular basis for a while and see how it affects your experience of the world, then decide if this is something you would like to add to the dance you are doing with the Cosmos.

INTERNAL DIALOG

We have 10,000 thoughts a day…and 8,000 of them are the same thoughts we had yesterday.

— Buddhist saying

Our internal dialog is the constant flow of thoughts we have about the world and about our self as we move through the day. While this flow of thoughts may contain visual images, for many of us it also contains a flow of comments we silently make to ourselves that echo our evaluation of what is happening. I would like to begin this chapter by belittling this internal dialog and then when I'm finished, I'll come to its defense.

If you spend time monitoring your own internal dialog you may find it to be a humbling experience. One way of monitoring your internal dialog is to say all of your thoughts out loud for several minutes (I recommend you do this somewhere private so you don't get hauled away as crazy). When I have done this, I have been appalled by the mundane inanity of my thoughts. It is like discovering that I have a banal and cliché-ridden sports announcer giving a running commentary on my life.

A problem with the internal dialog is that it takes our awareness away from *experiencing* reality and focuses it instead on our *interpretation* of reality. When we are heavily into internal dialog, we experience the world through a thick layer of interpretation, attending to the meaning we have assigned to what is happening rather than to what is actually going on. When we do that, we miss opportunities to notice how the world differs from what we expect. The internal dialog often takes us away from the present moment to rehash what has happened in the past (justifying how we feel about it or what we should have done differently or what we wished had happened); or it may focus on the future (perhaps running through various scenarios and how we will react, or simply looking with dread or tedium to what is coming up). It also takes us away from attending to what is going on immediately around us in favor of some distant locale (e.g., thinking about work when I am with my family).

Every meditative approach with which I am familiar involves attending to something other than our internal dialog. Attending to our internal dialog, however, is so habitual that after a few seconds of putting our consciousness somewhere else, we may find that we have drifted back into thinking rather than experiencing. My strategy, when I notice I have gone back to my internal dialog, is just to smile to myself and gently pull my consciousness back to the focus of the meditation. That, and a lot of practice have helped me to quiet the chatter in my head. One of the main improvements that happens with extended practice at meditating is the ability to spend longer and longer time periods free of internal dialog. Even then, I find there are some days when turning off my internal dialog is like trying to ignore a marching band passing a few feet away.

I mention all this for those of you who are experimenting with the Andean meditations and who don't have much experience with meditating. Be gentle and forgiving with yourself. If you like the experiences, if they touch you at some meaningful level, then persevere with patience. The experiences get deeper with practice. If not, well, there is no moral imperative within the Andean Cosmovision that you should continue on its path.

When learning to meditate, a lot of the effort involves turning off the internal dialog so that we can attend to the focus of the meditation. Our internal dialog, however, is not a bad thing and it is an incredibly useful part of us. To survive in our society we need to be able to interpret reality in a similar way to other people in our society. The internal dialog springs from our intellect, our yachay, and that is a valuable aspect of our existence. It is my yachay that convinces me I need to get up in the morning, go to the store, save money to go to Peru, mend a spat I've had with a friend, take my vitamins, go to work, and so on. It is just that if I operate on autopilot, then my internal dialog—my yachay—makes up 99% of my experience, and there is so much more to explore, so many other ways of understanding and being in this Cosmos.

MEDITATION: WHO AM I?

To me, at least, this seems a rather advanced meditation, partly because it builds upon other meditations but also because the experience can be quite profound. I like to prepare myself for this meditation by doing the following: I go to some place in Nature where I am unlikely to be disturbed; when I sit down I do the Touching Pachamama meditation to get out of my head and into the here-and-now; and then I do the Releasing Hucha meditation to clear my energy. After releasing my hucha I like to perform a small ritual of ayni (reciprocity) for Nature and the Cosmos. I pour a few drops of tequila onto the Pachamama and if I'm sitting next to a river, I give a few drops to my brother the river, and then I fling some into the sky for the Apus. I do all this with the intent of expressing my gratitude and respect for them and with the desire that they benefit from the energy of the offering. As a final preparatory step, I do the Tuning the Three Centers of Being meditation to ready the three centers for the following meditation. While it is worth the time to prepare for this meditation, the meditation itself is really quite simple.

Before you begin this meditation notice your energy, how it feels to be you right now.

Begin by sitting (on the ground or in a chair) with your spine comfortably erect (this meditation involves a vertical flow of energy, so it is useful to be aligned that way with the Pachamama and the Cosmos). I usually close my eyes. Take a few comfortable, full breaths and pay attention to your breathing as you do. Then move on to the following.

1) Ask yourself "Who am I?" Take a somewhat fuller than normal breath and with the out breath use your intent to move your consciousness from your head into your llankay (located slightly below your navel and a few inches within your body). As you breathe back in, use that in breath to pull energy from the outside world into your llankay. With subsequent breaths, feel the energy flow into and out of your llankay. Then simply be your llankay, notice the quality of energy in your llankay, get a sense of what it is like to be connected to the world from there. It may seem strange to talk about moving your consciousness to another part of your body other than your head, but that is the best way I have of describing what you are doing with your intent. Play with it and see what happens. The experience gets deeper with practice.

2) After spending some time in your llankay, ask yourself again "Who am I?" Take a somewhat fuller than normal breath, and with the in breath draw your consciousness from your llankay up to your munay (located in your heart) and then breathe out through your munay. With subsequent breaths feel the energy flow into and out of your munay. Simply be in your munay for a while, experiencing what it is like to perceive and interact with the Cosmos from there. Notice how the energy of your munay is different from that of your llankay.

3) Next, ask yourself again "Who am I?" Take a somewhat fuller than normal breath, and with the in breath move your consciousness from your munay to your yachay (located at the crown of your head) and be your yachay. Spend some time with your consciousness in your yachay, experiencing what it is like to be connected to and perceiving the Cosmos from there. Notice the difference in the quality of the energy in the yachay compared to the munay and the llankay.

4) And finally, when you have gotten in touch with the experience of being your yachay, you can move on to the fourth and final step. With your intent, enter into the profound silence of

the Cosmos…and transcend. No further instructions possible or necessary.

When you are finished savoring what that is like, open your eyes and return. Notice your energy and how you feel now. That is the meaning and effect of this meditation.

Give yourself some time to develop your skill with this meditation. At first you may have only an inkling of having moved your consciousness to another center and only the slightest taste of how that affects your consciousness. If this is intriguing enough to keep you going, then return to this meditation from time to time to more fully explore what it has to offer, which turns out to be a lot.

This meditative process reflects on a general pattern in the Andean Cosmovision. First we have a chance to explore new facets of our Being, then we move beyond being a collection of facets to being the diamond that has those facets.

Bon appétit.

FALLACIES

"The subjective fallacy is: 'If it works for me then it will work for everyone'.

The objective fallacy is: 'If it works for me then I can get anyone to believe that it works for me'."

From the delightful book: *Zen Without Zen Masters*, Camden Benares (1977), New Falcon Publications

ALL THE WORLD IS A STAGE

All the world's a stage, and we are merely players. But who is our intended audience: our society or the vast, mysterious Cosmos?

—William Shakespeare and don Américo Yábar

LIVING YOUR LIFE

"Let your life be a work of art."

—Américo Yábar

NOT DOING

"Just go out in Nature and 'not do', especially 'not do' thinking. If the power permits, that is all you have to do. There is no process to do. There are just vibrations, your energy and the energy of Nature and how your energy begins to change when you do this. That's it. I recommend that you do this a lot."

(Américo Yábar, personal communication)

I did it a lot ... and still do.

I think that a little elaboration on this meditation may be in order. Begin by situating yourself in Nature, not in a garden shaped by human thought but in a place of natural beauty and salka. Once there settle down and get comfortable; with your intent (sincere pretending) open up the energy field of your body so that it can merge with the energy of that place, and then...don't do.

Ok, so that requires a little explanation. What we normally "do" is to be aware of the interpretation of reality given to us by our mind. Our mind is continuously interpreting what is going on around us, categorizing and giving meaning to what we perceive, thinking about what is going on, or drifting off to think about other places and other times. Attending to the mind's interpretation of reality is the continuous 'doing' of our lives.

During this meditation, don't do that. Instead move your consciousness away from the products of your mind (perceptions, emotions, and thoughts) and be aware of your consciousness itself. Let go of thought and become aware of your own presence. Stop doing, and just be aware of being. You may have moments where your being doesn't stop at your skin.

I said it was simple, I didn't say it was easy. If at the beginning you can accomplish this only for a brief moment off and on during the time you spend meditating that is still great, each moment is an expansion of your awareness of the totality of who you are and of your relationship with Nature and the Cosmos.

Most of the other Andean meditations have a specific intent, but this does not. The effect of this meditation has slowly emerged within me over years of sporadic practice. The effect is incredible and beautiful. More than anything else, this meditation has been my convincer that love and beauty are inherent in Nature and the Cosmos.

ON DOING NOT DOING

Out beyond ideas…there is a field, I'll meet you there.

—Sufi mystic Jelaluddin Rumi (1207–1273)

I first ran into the concept of not doing in the works of Carlos Castaneda. His early books, particularly *Journey to Ixtlan* and *Tales of Power*, had a big effect on me when I was a young man. Later in my life, I ran into not doing again when I began working with don Américo. More recently, I have run across it in the works of Eckhart Tolle. In the previous chapter I shared the basic outline of how and where to practice 'not doing' as part of the Andean approach for exploring our relationship with Nature and the Cosmos. In this chapter I would like to express more about what I think not doing is all about and also share some techniques for not doing that I have found to be useful.

My awareness is almost always focused upon the products of my mind. The mind is an incredible thing; it takes all of the information reaching the senses and gives meaning to it all. That we see the world as consisting of separate objects rather than one undifferentiated mishmash of colors is thanks to the mind. Not only does my mind figure out, for example, that the chair I am looking at is an object separate from everything around it, it also places the object into the category of chair, so that when I look at the chair I don't see just an 'it', I see a chair. That's amazing when you think about it, and the mind is doing this *all of the time* we are awake with *everything* that we perceive. And that is just the start. Not only does the mind identify and label everything reaching our sense organs, it also figures out–of all the millions of things happening around us at any one moment–what is the most important thing for us to be paying attention to at any particular moment.

The mind also makes judgements about the good or bad of what is happening and how what is going on relates to our view of ourselves and of the people around us and of the world. The mind also likes to wander away from what is happening here and now, to consider instead what has happened in the past or what might happen in the future or what might be happening elsewhere. The workings of the mind are accompanied by our internal dialog, a flow of thoughts that accompanies the process of the mind making sense out of the world. Our normal state of awareness is to experience and act on the interpretation of the world that our mind presents to us. This is so much our habitual experience that we mistake the interpretation of reality presented to us by the mind as being reality itself. We think that the meaning of what is going on comes from what is out there, rather than being something our mind is creating in response to what is out there.

To say that our mind is massively useful would be a gross understatement. It is rather helpful when putting on your clothes to know what part of reality is you and what part of reality are your pants, and when eating to know what is food and what is not, and to know why you need to have a job and how to get there, and how the refrigerator opens, and that you need to look both ways before crossing the road, and so on and so on and so on and...well...everything we need to know to live in this world.

After acknowledging its indispensable utility, I'd like to point out that the mind is, like, totally mental (sorry...idiomatic joke). It can only give us its mentally created interpretation of reality, not reality itself. Reality itself is beyond all the thoughts, concepts, ideas, perceptions, and feelings we have about it. Reality is vastly more mysterious and wondrous than our mind's mental interpretation of it. And the same is true of us. You are the mysterious Being who has a mind, the Being from which a mind has emerged, not the limited being envisioned by your mind.

Knowing yourself deeply has nothing to do with any ideas, concepts, or beliefs you have about yourself. Knowing yourself deeply involves experiencing yourself at the level of Being.
— Eckhart Tolle (paraphrase)

In his book *A New Earth*, Tolle points out that we are not the experience created by our minds (our perceptions, our thoughts, our feelings). We are instead the experiencer, we are consciousness. Consciousness cannot be known, for it is the knower not what is known, and while we cannot know consciousness we can become aware of our existence as consciousness itself. We can sense it here and now as our very Presence. When we move our awareness to consciousness itself, we experience the world beyond/before/behind the interpretations of the mind. This is the basic dance step of the mystic.

While we cannot understand or talk about that which lies beyond all our mental constructs of reality, we can use words as guideposts to help us get there. Carlos Castaneda, don Américo, and Eckhart Tolle are all excellent sources for how to do just that. I have culled a variety of techniques from them that I have found to be useful and present some of my favorites below. On any one day, one technique seems to work better for me than the others, and it is useful to have several to try. And on some days, of course, nothing works. Here are some things to try (adapted from Tolle's book *A New Earth*):

- Move your consciousness away from the products of your mind (perceptions, emotions, and thoughts) and be aware of your consciousness itself. Let go of thought, become still and alert, and feel your own presence, become your own consciousness.

- Time is a construct of our mind, outside of the mind there lies eternity, defined not as an infinite length of time but as the state of timelessness not broken into past, present, and future. One way to 'not do' is to enter completely into Now. I played around with this for a while. A few times a day I would ask myself 'is it still now?', and then I would notice what my experience was like when I checked out whether it was indeed still now. I found that there is something always there in my experience when I check out 'now.' The mind can only interpret reality within a flow of time, it can't do its thing in pure now (eternity). Your consciousness exists in eternity.

- We can only perceive light because dark also exists. Without darkness, we could not see light. We can only hear sounds because silence also exists. Without silence, we could not hear sounds. There is an ever-present silence in our experience that is the background to the sounds we hear. Listen to that silence. This works very well for me, by the way, and not at all for my friend and that is just the way we are.

- Doing involves paying attention to the various forms (chairs, people, trees, rivers) that our mind creates out of raw reality. Let that go, experience what you experience before your mind has organized the world for you. Be aware of your existence as the container in which those forms arise.

- When my internal dialog has the bit in its teeth and has taken off, I find it very difficult to enter the now, and I have found the following steps help me get started. I like to do this while I am taking a walk.
    - I start by paying exquisite attention to my breathing. I can't do that fully and keep my mental internal dialog going at the same time. I do this for a minute or two.

 – After paying attention to my breathing for a
   while, I pay attention to the living energy of my
   body, the sensations that inform me that my body
   is indeed still here and alive. It is kind of a gentle
   tingling within the body but not really tingling…
   just check it out to see what I mean.
 – And after that, I either slip completely into the
   experience of now or listen to the silence.

There is a particular beauty and significance to practicing not
doing in Nature. It is as if my existence becomes greater than my
body. As I merge with Nature, who I am begins to change in a way
that brings more salka and beauty into my existence.

PACHA AND THE
THREE WORLDS

This chapter will serve as a conceptual foundation for one of my favorite meditations from the Andes. The meditation involves connecting with the three levels of existence, the three worlds, of the Andean Cosmovision. They are the *uju pacha* (lower world), the *kay pacha* (surface world) and the *janaq pacha* (upper world). I have given these Quechua words the spelling they would have if written in Spanish. The pronunciation in English is roughly: ukhu pacha, kie pacha, and hanak pacha.

Like all of the meditations I have shared so far, the meditation involving the three worlds is quite simple. As I began exploring it, however, I found that I wanted to have a better understanding of what the meditation was all about. In searching my notes, I found only the briefest descriptions from Américo concerning the uju pacha, kay pacha, and janaq pacha. I decided to turn to what literature is available on the Andean Cosmovision to see if I could flesh out my understanding of these terms. What I found has helped me to hone my intent with the meditations and I would like to share it with you.

The three worlds of uju pacha, kay pacha, and janaq pacha are so fundamental to the Andean Cosmovision that there is actually a fair amount of information in the academic literature concerning how the Andean people interpret these terms. These interpretations, however, vary widely across the sources I have found.

Some of the breadth of meaning of the three terms can be attributed to the 500 years of Christian influence on the Andean culture. It takes no great conceptual leap to link the uju pacha (the lower world) with the Christian concept of hell and the janaq pacha (the upper world) with the Christian concept of heaven, and this has changed the meaning of the terms in the post-conquest culture. Even the Q'ero, the people with whom I have worked and who are viewed by many as being among the purer keepers of the flame of the indigenous Andean Cosmovision, readily identify themselves as being Christian (see Wilcox, 2004). What the Q'ero exactly mean by this is hard to say, for they have blended Christianity with the Andean Cosmovision. It brings to mind the times I have heard women in a remote village of Peru singing about "Jesus the Sacred Mountain".

If we look at the conceptualization of the three worlds that predates the Christian conquest of the Andes, then a very different understanding emerges. Even then, however, there are still some differences among sources concerning how these terms are to be interpreted. When faced with a multitude of interpretations of the nature of the uju pacha, kay pacha, and janaq pacha, What did I do? I picked the one I liked, the one that best fit my own understanding of the Andean Cosmovision, and, ultimately, the one that enhanced the power of the meditation.

The following description of the nature of the uju pacha, kay pacha, and janaq pachca is based upon the chapter "Andean Cosmology and Cosmography in the North-Peruvian Shamanic Mesa", written by Mario Polia, in the book *Mesas & Cosmologies in the Central Andes*, edited by Douglas Sharon (2006). An understanding of these three terms depends upon an understanding of the word pacha.

The Quechua word *pacha* does not correspond directly to any term or concept we have in the West. It is, instead, an integration of our concepts of place, time, and consciousness. One facet of pacha encompasses the concept of space/earth/world/

place. We have already in this book run across Pachamama as the great Being who is the planet Earth. A second facet of pacha involves the concept of time/era/period. The Quechua term *tarpui pacha*, for example, refers to the correct time for the sowing of seeds. Pacha thus encompasses both space/earth/world/place and time/era/period, in other words space/time. The third element involved in pacha is consciousness. In the Andean Cosmovision, consciousness is an inherent, immanent, aspect of the Cosmos. Consciousness cannot be bound by any concept, including those of space and time, so in essence it exists both within and outside space and time. When we talk about a particular time and space, consciousness will be there as well.

In terms of a world or location or place, the uju pacha is the lower world, the world below, the interior world, a place associated with the depths of the planet. When the Andean people want to communicate with the uju pacha, they may go to a spring or to a crack in the earth's surface that provides a conduit into the interior of the world. The uju pacha is the deeply interior world. Closer to the surface is the urin pacha, where seeds are planted to take root and grow. The uju pacha and urin pacha also refer to time: in this case, the distant past (uju pacha) and the recent past (urin pacha). The uju pacha is the time of our ancestors and before. The urin pacha is the time when seeds were planted in our lives that have blossomed into who we have recently become, who we are now, and who we are about to become. For the purpose of meditation, I don't draw a distinction between the uju pacha (distant past and deeply interior) and the urin pacha (more recent past and not so deeply interior), and simply call them both the uju pacha (the past and interior world).

A connection with the uju pacha is accomplished by connecting to the interior world (e.g., the interior of the planet). When we do that, we also connect with the past. Consciousness exists outside all our mind's constructs of space and time, so our consciousness is in the uju pacha just like it is here and now.

The kay pacha is the surface world, the world in which we live. The kay pacha is also the present time, not necessarily this exact moment at the cutting edge of now, but the general neighborhood of time around it. I like to refer to it as the now-ish. Of course, our consciousness is here with us in the kay pacha.

The third world, the *janaq pacha*, is the superior world, the world above. The near above, the realm of the Beings who are the majestic mountain peaks (the *Apus*), is known as the *janan pacha*. The *janaq* pacha is the highest zone, the realm of the stars that serve as "the seat of archetypal forms of spiritual principle of all living things" (Polia, pg 35). I love that definition. You might want to read it again and savor it. The janan pacha and janaq pacha also refer to the future, the near and distant future respectively. Again, in my meditations I drop the distinction between the janan and janaq pacha and simply refer to the superior/future world as the janaq pacha. Connection with the janaq pacha is accomplished by connecting to the sky above, possibly as far as the stars themselves, or even beyond to Mama Tuta (the dark, the void, who holds the stars in her embrace), and this is tied intrinsically to connecting with the future. Our consciousness resides in the future as well.

Connecting with the uju pacha connects us to our interior world and to the past that has led us to who we are now. Connecting with the kay pacha connects us to the world around us and who we are now. Connecting to the janaq pacha connects us to the superior world and draws us towards our future as archetypal forms of the spiritual principle of all living things. Our consciousness exists across all of those places and times, unfettered by the concepts of space and time.

MEDITATION: CONNECTING THE THREE WORLDS

In the previous chapter I introduced the three worlds of the Andean Cosmovision: the uju pacha, the kay pacha, and the janaq pacha. In this chapter I would like to share a meditation that involves evoking a conscious connection with those worlds.

Before doing this meditation, I like to prepare my internal state, adjust my energy, to create a good foundation for the meditation. I usually begin by doing the Touching Pachamama meditation, which just takes a few minutes. I then clean my energy with the Releasing Hucha meditation, which also takes just a few minutes. Of course, the neat thing is that these preparatory mediations are themselves very beneficial over the long run and simple though they are they can take you far down the Andean path.

It is also important when doing these meditations to remember that, while they may serve as processes for personal transformation, this transformation is just the byproduct of something more fundamental: a shift in our relationship with Nature and the Cosmos. Ayni (reciprocity) is the guiding principle of that relationship. Whenever possible, I do these meditations outside in Nature, and I bring along an offering (usually a little tequila) to give in gratitude to the Pachamama and the Apus to complete the circle of ayni, for they are intimately involved in this meditation as well.

When you are ready to proceed, then I recommend you spend a moment surveying your energy, noticing what it feels like to be you right now. The meaning of the meditation is the effect it has on you, and to explore that, you need to compare how you feel before you start to how you feel when you have finished.

You can do this meditation either standing or sitting on the ground but I prefer to stand.

Begin by getting in touch with the uju pacha. Gesture toward the earth and with your intent (sincere pretending) send filaments of your energy from your hands down into the deep interior of the Pachamama, saying "Uju pacha" (pronounced "ukhu pacha") aloud as you do this. With your intent connect not only with the deep interior of the Pachamama but also with the deep interior of time, with the distant past, the origin of things. Then bring your intent slowly towards the surface of Pachamama and connect with the less distant past, with the ancestors. Finally bring it to just below the surface and connect to the more recent past where the seeds where planted that blossomed into who you are now. Play around with this for a bit, taking the time to experience this connection with the interior world and the past.

Now, move your hands up to your chest and then spread them out horizontally as if to say "Here I am now" and connect to the surface world and the present time spread out before you, the world in which we are living now. Say "Kay pacha" (pronounced "kie pacha") as you do this. Use your intent to connect to the world around you and who you are at the present moment. Again, take your time to get into this.

Finally, throw your hands up to the sky and send the filaments of your energy through your finger tips shooting up toward the Cosmos, saying "Janaq pacha" (pronounced "hanak pacha"). Use your intent to not only connect to the Cosmos above but also to the future, all the way up to the stars that contain the blueprint of the perfect archetypical spiritual Being towards which you are evolving. You may feel the stars reaching down to pull you up to that future.

That is what I do to get set up for the meditation.

The following is best done with a good deal of panache, it is also particularly fun and powerful to do it with a group of people.

Throw your hands down toward the ground and call out "Uju pacha". Grab the energy from the uju pacha and pull it quickly into your chest and exclaim "Kay pacha". Then throw the energy into the sky as you shout "Janaq pacha!!" Do this quickly, only spending a second at each world. Pause for a couple of seconds and do the process again, then a third time, and a fourth time. Adding more energy each time until the fourth "Janaq pacha" skyrockets with enthusiasm into the Cosmos.

Now notice how you feel immediately after you have finished. Savor it. It leaves me feeling elongated in time, as if I am conscious of my 'long body' (the me that exists through the passage of time), but whatever effect it has on you is the meaning of the meditation for you, and you can decide if it has value for you.

GIVING FLOWERS TO THE COSMOS

We have looked at several meditations that serve as portals for exploring untapped facets of who we are as human beings living in this Cosmos. I would like to bring us back to consider the wider context of the Andean Cosmovision, which is our relationship with Nature and the Cosmos, a relationship guided by the Andean principle of ayni (reciprocity).

The importance of ayni in the Andean Cosmovision is not easy to grasp with Western thought, for it is essentially about relationship while we in the West tend to focus instead on outcomes. It is easy to look at the various meditations I am sharing and think of the Andean Cosmovision as primarily a way to achieve various beneficial effects for ourselves. The meditations, however, are like steps in a beautiful dance, and if we don't also pay attention to the partner we are dancing with (the Cosmos) and to the music itself, then we miss the essence and much of the potential power and beauty of the Andean Cosmovision. While the meditations have an immediate and beneficial effect, I have come to realize over the years that something else gradually emerges. Like a flower slowly blossoming a transformation arises within us as a result of being in a loving and mutually supportive relationship with Nature and the Cosmos.

The primary way I have for nourishing this relationship is through acts of gratitude known as *despachos*[1]. Simple despachos have become an ever-present part of my Andean meditative practice. At first I offered despachos mainly because I had an intellectual understanding that ayni is a fundamental principle of the Andean Cosmovision. As I entered more fully into the Andean Cosmovision, however, I began to have moments of being overcome with appreciation of living in a conscious Cosmos, a Cosmos where the Pachamama accepts our hucha from us, where the Cosmos gives us refined energy to replace the hucha, and where all the facets of Nature and the Cosmos are available to help support our personal and interpersonal transformations. My despachos eventually became a matter of delight.

I always bring a little alcohol with me when I go into the canyons to meditate. After clearing my hucha, I pour a few drops onto the Pachamama with the intent that it carry my gratitude to her. If I am sitting next to a creek I give a little to the creek with the same intent, and I spew a little into the sky for the Apus. These acts–the simplest of despachos–are my heartfelt way of nourishing my relationship with Nature and the Cosmos.

It is important to me that you understand the underlying nature of a despacho. A despacho is not the material component of a spell to control Nature, nor is it a bribe or payment to Nature for services rendered. Giving a despacho is like giving flowers to a loved one; it is an act that celebrates and elevates a loving relationship. It is in essence an energetic act, giving energy in the form of love as part of the circle of ayni. The beauty of ayni is that, unlike giving a store money in exchange for a fishing rod, it leaves both parties feeling like they have more energy than when they started. This extra energy arises from the nature of the relationship; it is like a spiral where every completion of the circle of ayni lifts both parties a little higher.

Occasionally I like to offer a more elaborate despacho, and this takes a little bit of preparation. I base these despachos on a few of the elements I have seen go into the very elaborate and beautiful despachos made by the Q'ero paqos in Peru. For a despacho to the Pachamama, I bring three red flowers and three white flowers. Red and white flowers are an important part of almost all Andean despachos. Red flowers represent blood, the Pachamama, the feminine. White flowers represent masculine energy, the snow on the Apus, and the stars. I also add three sugar cubes or three pieces of candy for the Pachamama. Once when I was in Peru, a Q'ero woman was describing to me the significance of the various elements she was adding to her despacho. She placed some candy into the despacho and explained that the Pachamama has a sweet tooth. Américo, who was translating for us, grinned and added that this might be a projection. Still, candy or sweets are a nice touch for a despacho to the Pachamama.

To complete the despacho for the Pachamama I dig a small hole into the earth. In the Andes the despacho would be wrapped in a large sheet of paper and tied with a string before burying, but I usually skip the paper for Western reasons (so that there will be less to biodegrade). Before putting the flowers into the ground, I hold them up to my lips and gently blow on them three times with the intent of connecting my filaments to the flowers and imbuing them with the very finest of my energy. I then gently place the sugar cubes and the flowers into the hole and pour a little alcohol on them while holding the intent of expressing my gratitude to the Pachamama for all that she gives us. Finally, I fill in the dirt on top of the despacho and gently press it down with my hands. With my intent, I send the energy of the despacho to Pachamama in gratitude.

For the creek that flows past my meditation spot I bring three red and three white flowers, gently blow on them three times to imbue them with my filaments and the very finest of my energy, and then I cast the flowers into the flowing water. I follow this with a little alcohol, again with the intent of expressing my gratitude to my brother the creek, for the beauty that he brings to my life, and for what he gives me when I meditate with him.

For the Apus, I use the same elements as I do for a despacho for the Pachamama but I bury the despacho in the slopes of the

Apu. If I'm not actually at the Apu, I put the elements in a piece of paper, tied with a string, which I then place in a fire. As it burns I use my intent to send the energy of the despacho to the Apu. Giving a despacho to an Apu with a fire is more traditional than burying it, but I am not very often in a place where a fire would be welcome.

This is just the starting point on how to create despachos. Sometimes I want to do something really special. The last time I made a despacho for an Apu, for example, I added cotton fluff to represent the clouds, a small hummingbird figurine (hummingbirds are the messengers of the Apus), a small piece of silver accompanied by my apology for the silver mining that had occurred in the past in the Apu, a small rainbow bead to represent the rainbow that connects the Apu to Pachamama, a yellow flower to represent Tai Tai Inti (the sun), and so on.

The paqos of the Andes make very elaborate despachos indeed, containing dozens of elements selected with specific intent and arranged in a beautiful mandala-like design. The despachos and the ceremonies and the people themselves are incredibly beautiful and touching and loving. We can honor and love that they are that way, and we don't have to be exactly like them. One of the most beautiful despacho ceremonies I have attended was with don Américo and a group of people on the slopes of a volcano in Hawaii. We all brought some flowers and arranged them there on the breast of the Pachamama and connected with her with the intent of expressing our gratitude. A shaft of sunlight sprang through the clouds and illuminated just the despacho. It doesn't get much better than that.

For the past summer I have meditated a lot outdoors, and I have gotten a lot from the meditations, and I've given many despachos, and it is all ayni, all reciprocity, given with respect and love. I've changed, my experience of reality has changed, the reality around me has changed, all in subtle ways, but enough for my heart to sing a soft melody. Ayni lies at the heart of that experience.

— END NOTE —

[1.] Joan Wilcox in her informative book, *Masters of the Living Energy: The Mystical World of the Q'ero of Peru*, draws a distinction between *despachos* (made for specific outcomes) and *pagos* (simple expressions of gratitude). Both terms are Spanish in origin, and when I turn to my English-Spanish dictionary to see if it can clarify the meaning of the terms, I am led to wonder how either ever came to be associated with the offerings made in the Andes.

I asked don Américo about this, and he said that perhaps a better term to use for a despacho of gratitude would be the ancient Quechua term *haywarisca*. The term despacho, however, is so ingrained in both the Western understanding of the Andean Cosmovision and in my own mind that I just stick with it. For more information about making despachos I recommend Joan Wilcox's book.

MEDITATION: SAIWACHAKUY (DOWNWARD)

This is a meditation I described earlier in this book (as the 'Love to Pachamama' meditation). I wanted you to have it then as it is such a simple and effective way to give people a taste of the Andean Cosmovision. Now that we have some more experiences and concepts under our belts, I would like to return to it. I learned this meditation from don Américo, but he didn't give it a name. It appears to fit the definition of a *saiwachakuy* as described by Joan Wilcox in her book, *Masters of the Living Energy*, so I am calling it that. Another version of saiwachakuy will be covered in a later chapter.

Joan describes a saiwachakuy as a column of energy that connects the three worlds of the janaq pacha, kay pacha, and uju pacha. The Connecting the Three Worlds meditation covered earlier moves the energy from the uju pacha up to the janaq pacha, while this meditation moves the energy in the opposite direction from the janaq pacha down to the uju pacha.

I usually begin this mediation by first doing the Touching Pachamama and Releasing Hucha meditations. The meditation then proceeds as described below. I like to do this while sitting on the Pachamama.

With intent (sincere pretending), open the energy center at the crown of your head and let the refined energy of the Cosmos flow down through your head and into your munay. When the energy enters your munay, use your intent to transform the energy into love. Then, open up the energy center at the bottom of your spine and let the love flow into the Pachamama. For as long as you like, sit there and serve as the conduit of energy from the Cosmos to the Pachamama, transforming the energy into love as it flows through your munay.

In addition to the pleasant effects the meditation has on me I get a sense while I am doing it that it is an act of love for the Pachamama and the Cosmos, and further, that they appreciate it, that this is somehow a service to them. I feel part of something grand, a poetic salka movement on this planet, a re-awakening of the human race to a long lost and beautiful relationship with Nature and the Cosmos. Your experience, of course, will be whatever it is. Play with it and see what happens.

This meditation is one of the ways I respond when I hear of something horrible my species has just done to our Pachamama. I don't, however, limit expressing my love to those I love just to those times when they are hurt.

MEDITATION:
SHEDDING HUCHA

As a reminder, hucha is heavy, discordant, chaotic energy. It arises within us when our society or our ego place demands upon us that take us out of harmony with our natural state of being. Hucha is not evil or bad, it is just heavy and discordant, and getting rid of it leaves us with more lightness of Being.

We looked at one way of getting rid of our hucha in the meditation Releasing Hucha (which is my favorite way). The Shedding Hucha meditation provides a quicker way of doing the same thing. Quick is not necessary a virtue, but it does make it easy to do this routinely after work or before interacting with someone who may be vulnerable to your hucha (e.g., a client) or after absorbing someone else's hucha (e.g., a client). Here is how it goes.

While standing, raise both your arms above your head with the palms of your hands facing the sky. With intent (sincere pretending), connect to the energy of the Cosmos with your right hand and let that energy flow into and accumulate in your right hand. When you feel the energy gathered into your right hand, slowly bring your two palms together (still over your head) and with intent let the energy flow through your right hand into your left hand. From your left hand let the energy flow down your left arm and into your heart (munay). When the energy flows into your heart, transform the energy into love and let it radiate out from your munay into the rest of your body.

Now, bring your hands down to the top of your head and then slowly move your hands down over your body from head to toes with the intent of gathering up all your hucha from your body with your hands (like a vacuum cleaner). When you get to your toes, put your palms down on the Pachamama and ask her to absorb all the hucha from your hands. One of the great gifts the Pachamama gives us is to accept our hucha and recycle it into refined energy. This is part of the circle of ayni that we nourish when we express our gratitude to the Pachamama in the form of despachos.

Do this process slowly enough to maintain the intent of what you are doing. If you do it too quickly, it can become a mechanical process without intent and will lose its quality. Still, this is something that doesn't take very long and you will find that over time you can do it more quickly and still hold your intent. Back when I had a more stressful job I would routinely do this in my garage after arriving home and before entering my house to be with my family.

YANANTIN
(THE COMPLEMENTARITY
OF OPPOSITES)

The basic idea of the complementarity of opposites is that opposite concepts define each other, and in fact, they cannot exist without each other. Dark, for example, defines light and light defines dark. If only light existed then we would not understand dark, and without dark to contrast it with we would not understand light either. A similar relationship exists between the sunny side and the shady side of a mountain. If there is a sunny side of a mountain, there must also be a shady side. If all the mountain is in sun, then there is no sunny side and shady side; if all the mountain is in shade, there is no shady side and sunny side. The sunny side and shady side of a mountain define each other and cannot exist without each other. Good and evil define each other and rely upon each other to exist. If only good existed we would not understand evil, and without evil to contrast it to we would not understand good. Up and down, left and right, introverted and extroverted, happy and sad are other examples of complementary opposites.

I first ran into the concept of the complementarity of opposites in my study of Taoism when I was a young man. For many years, Taoism served as my favorite philosophy of the dynamics of the Cosmos, but I could never get a handle on how to move it from being a philosophy to applying it in my life. The indigenous Andean culture, however, is organized around this principle.

In the Andes the complementarity of opposites is called *yanantin*. Yanantin not only informs many of the meditations, it also permeates the entire Andean Cosmovision. I would like to take a few chapters to explore this in some detail. In this first chapter I will cover the basics of the complementarity of opposites, introduced from the perspective of Taoism.

In Taoism, the primary complementary and opposite energies of the Cosmos are yin and yang; they define each other and can only exist together. The complementary natures of yin and yang are expressed in a variety of ways, such as female/male, dark/light, yielding/aggressive, intuitive/logical, and so on. The following familiar Taoist image is often used to express the relationship between yin and yang (see Figure 1).

The circle as a whole represents the Cosmos, which is divided into the com-

Figure 1

plementary energies of yin and yang, represented by the dark and light pollywogs of the circle respectively. The two smaller circles (of black within the white and white within the black) show that yin and yang are not absolutes, that a situation that is very yin also contains a germ of yang and a situation that is very yang also contains a germ of yin.

It is clear in looking at the figure that the dark and light parts define each other, the boundary of one area establishes the boundary of the other. That there is a distinction (a boundary) between the two is important, for without a boundary between white and black we get the following (Figure 2), which I like to call the "undifferentiated grayness of the void", where neither white nor black exist. It is also significant that the boundary between yin and yang in Figure 1 is curved. The boundary could

Figure 2

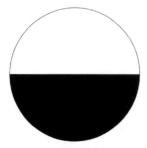

Figure 3

be drawn as simply a straight line (Figure 3), but drawing the line as a curve suggests movement. The two pollywogs of yin and yang are dancing around each other, for the Cosmos is not static but *always* flowing and changing, yin and yang dancing together.

And now we get to something really important: when we divide the Cosmos into pollywogs dancing with each other, then something new emerges that is created by the dance. This something is not found in the undifferentiated void of the circle, nor is it found if the two complementary aspects of the Cosmos are inert and do not interact. It arises only from the dance. In systems theory this is called an emergent property. In everyday language we describe an emergent property as the whole being greater than the sum of the parts.

The magic of emergent properties can be quite amazing. Let's say that we take a bunch of individual molecules and write down what each can do. Then, we put the molecules together in the form of a single cell organism and write down what the cell can do: it can swim, it can reproduce, it can live. Those are all emergent properties that arise from the molecules working (dancing) together. Molecules by themselves, outside the dance, cannot do those things.

So, when the Cosmos is divided into two dynamic opposites that dance together, then something special emerges from each dance. Some of the complementary opposites that play an important role in the Andean Cosmovision are:

- male/female
- domesticated energy/undomesticated energy (*salka*)
- the vertical dimension/the horizontal dimension
- the energy on the right side of a person (*paña*)/the energy on the left side (*lloqe*)

- the energy of day/the energy of evening
- heavy energy (*hucha*)/light energy (*sami*)
- the traditional ways/the Christian ways
- the visible world (*kaylla*)/the invisible world (*tiqsi*).

These are not different names for the same way of dividing the circle (e.g., dividing the Cosmos into male and female energy does not also divide it into domesticated and undomesticated energy). They each, instead, represent a different way of dividing the circle into complementary opposites. In the next couple of chapters, I will share how the dance of these opposites shapes the Andean Cosmovision and how it sheds light on some of the meditations. It is a bit yachay and if you are not interested then skim over it, but it is important to me that I tell you about it.

WARMI-QHARI
(WOMAN/MAN)

The Andean Cosmovision embodies the complementarity of opposites in a way that informs the Andean people's relationship with Nature and the Cosmos, with each other, and with the various facets of their own Being. In this chapter, I would like to take a look at the role of the complementary opposites of female and male in the traditional Andean culture. The clear distinctions between the two and the bringing together of their disparate energies into a unified whole is fundamental to the Andean Cosmovision. While I find the relationship between males and females in the Andes to be fascinating on its own, I am offering it to you not as a blueprint for how we might want to handle the relationship between sexes in our culture but as a window to view how the complementarity of opposites can be embodied in life. The following information was culled from the writings of the anthropologists Inge Bolin and Catherine Allen (see the recommended readings at the end of this book), and it is also consistent with my own experiences in Peru.

In the traditional, indigenous, Andean culture, the differentiation of males and females is obvious. At community meetings, the males gather with the males and the females gather with the females. When visiting friends, males visit their male friends and females visit their female friends. The differentiation of female and male overlaps to some degree another important pair of complementary opposites in the the Andean Cosmovision: the horizontal and vertical dimensions (the metaphysical implications of the horizontal and vertical dimensions will be discussed in a later chapter). At the community meetings, the females array themselves in the horizontal dimension, sitting on the ground. This puts them in intimate physical contact with the Pachamama, the great mother who is the planet Earth. The men array themselves in a vertical orientation, sitting in chairs or standing, perhaps leaning against a wall. The horizontal and vertical dimensions also show up in their clothing. Stripes in the women's clothing are usually horizontal, while those of the men's are usually vertical. And, while both sexes weave, women traditionally work the horizontal loom while men work the vertical loom. The horizontal/vertical orientation also appears in their relationships with others of their sex. Relationships among the women are more egalitarian (horizontal) while those among the men are more likely to incorporate the hierarchical (vertical) nature of their political and social roles within the community.

There are many other differentiations between the roles of the sexes as well. When planting, it is the male's task to break open the ground with a foot plow and the female's to plant the seed (if a woman does not plant the seed, then it will not grow). While men have the title of head of the household, women have authority over most aspects of actually running the household (which is their domain). The men's domain is that of the relationship between the household and the outside world. It is, for example, the male's task to transport the crops from field to market and to travel to other villages when necessary. The men speak for the family at community meetings, but they express views that have been agreed to by both the husband and the wife.

In the Inca empire, the emperor and the empress were of equal power, each being the leader of distinct, complementary aspects of their culture. In the Inca capital city of Cusco, the upper city was the domain of the emperor and the lower city was the domain of the empress. In addition to serving as leaders of complementary aspects of the culture, they also served complementary roles in the culture's relationship with the Cosmos. The emperor was the head of a male lineage that had the sun at its apex, while the empress was the head of a female lineage that had the moon at its apex. In the Andes today men and women often play equal but parallel roles in sacred ceremonies, working side by side but working in different spiritual domains.

While the traditional Andean culture draws a very clear boundary between female activities and male activities, this surprisingly does not lead to a corresponding rigidity in what people are allowed to do. Men are allowed to do female activities and women are allowed to do male activities. Working the horizontal loom, for example, is clearly defined as a woman's activity, but men can work the horizontal loom if they choose. The same holds for the vertical loom, it is a clearly a man's device but women may use it as well. During the time of the Inca empire, when the emperor left the city to go to war, the empress would step in to fulfill his duties (and the Inca army contained some women warriors). A woman may take on a man's role, which she does she does in a feminine way. A man may take on a woman's role, which he does in a masculine way. There is room for a germ of male in the female and for a germ of female in the male.

The two complementary opposites of female and male are clearly defined in the Andes. When masculine and feminine energy dance together, something new emerges. A marriage in the Andes is known as a *warmi-qhari* which is literally translated as *woman-man*. The warmi-qhari is a bringing into harmony of two complementary energies (yanantin) into something that is greater than the sum of the parts. In this fusion, the boundaries between female and male do not disappear; being separate but dancing together is required for emergent properties to appear. In the traditional Andean culture, when a wife and husband are feeling particularly affectionate towards each other they may trade insults or toss small stones or sticks at each other. To me, it is as if the Andean couple are reinforcing that they are a conjunction of complementary opposites, while celebrating their union.

"These sets of complementary contrasts—flexible and context-dependent run through every aspect of life in the Andean community; they provide the framework within which the Runakuna (the Andean people) think and act. It is difficult to translate them into English terminology without giving the impression of a set of absolute, static oppositions. The relativity characteristic of Andean thinking involves the continual enfolding of male and female principles that both contain and exclude each other. Each individual can provide the male or female element of another pairing to form another individual, a microcosm of a higher order. Thus, while each man or woman is a complete individual with both male and female qualities, the two unite to form another entity of a higher order: a warmi-qhari" (my edited version of Allen, pg. 64).

Each of us has male and female qualities, male and female energies. The masculine energy tends to be greater in males and the feminine energy tends to be greater in females. Yanantin is the harmony of those energies within us. I am reminded of something don Américo once said. "When we were young, we had a mother and father to guide us, each with their own different energy. Now that we are mature, it is time to call upon the mother and father within us to guide our own development." The mother and father within us are not echoes of our own parents, they are our connections to the perfect male and female energy of the Cosmos, and with intent we can call on them to help guide us.

TINKUY (EMERGENCE)

In this chapter, I would like to take a look at how the complementarity of opposites informs the relationships between the
indigenous communities in the Andes. The information comes
from the beautiful and insightful writings of the anthropologists
Inge Bolin and Catherine Allen, and it also passes my personal test
of fitting generally what I have witnessed in my own travels in Peru.
At the end of this chapter, I provide the page numbers of the relevant sections of Bolin's and Allen's books so that you can peruse
their original material yourself to get a more complete picture.

A good place to start is with the Andean festival of *Pukllay*.
Pukllay is held in the Andes in February over a period of eight
days. After the Spanish arrived, the festival was incorporated into
the Catholic celebration of Carnival, but it still contains strong
connections to its pre-Conquest roots. Pukllay is a time of singing and dancing, "Women dance with bundles of maize, grain,
and fruit in their shawls. Young mothers bundle in their infants
as well, who bounce wide-eyed above the maternal twirling and

stamping. Sometimes, women and
men form two choirs to sing back and
forth" (Allen, page 155). The festival is also a time of whipping dances,
teasing, and love making, a time
when the people are released from
their traditional restraints and can do
and express what cannot be done or
expressed at other times. Pukllay also

used to be the time of ritual battles (*Yawar Mayu*–river of blood) between neighboring communities.

The ritual battles of Pukllay were outlawed by the conquering Spanish but continued in the more remote regions of the Andes until recent times (within the living memory of Andeans interviewed by Catherine Allen). The battles were held at the boundaries between communities. The men from the two communities would fight each other while the women would sing songs encouraging their men to be brave and not to fear the river of blood. The battle could take various forms: the two sides might throw hard, unripe fruit at each other, or they might form opposing lines and strike each other with their warak'a (slings) or with staffs. It was important that some blood be spilled during the encounter as an offering to the Pachamama and to the Apus and to the various Sacred Sites. If a man died during the fight (an uncommon event but not unheard of), his body was buried there as a further offering to the sacred Beings.

What is amazing to me about these fights is the way they embodied an appreciation of the complementarity of opposites. The men engaged in these ceremonial conflicts bravely, facing the possibility of injury or even death, while being cheered on by the women; yet the fights were held for the betterment of the larger Andean community which encompassed both sides of the fight. The blood that was spilled as an offering to the Pachamama was for the fertility of the fields in *both* communities. It was in this way a communal effort, a conflict to benefit both sides, which from a Western perspective is a rather mind-boggling concept. "Blood had to flow," an Andean man told Bolin as he was recounting his participation in such battles, "Pachamama needs a few drops of blood, and we all come together to provide this offering. So we meet as opponents and end in solidarity" (Bolin, pg 95).

The fighting, while fierce and occasionally deadly, was not fueled by hostility. At the end of the battle, the men from opposing sides might give each other exaggerated hugs, then sacrifice a sheep together and settle down to a communal feast to celebrate their unity. If the point of this was to create a sense of larger community, then why fight each other? The reason was to reinforce the distinct identity of the two cultures, and to confirm their boundaries. "We must respect the borderlines," the same man told Bolin, "only then can we live together in harmony" (Bolin, pg 95).

On the flip side, if it is important that they fight each other in order to reinforce that they are separate entities, why then come together afterward to celebrate their union as one people? The answer is that this was the whole point of the ritual conflict. To embody the complementarity of opposites, the distinction between the two communities must be made clear, while at the same time they are brought together to form a single entity from which something greater than the sum of the two will emerge.

In the Andes, an encounter of differing energies, such as that of Yawar Mayu, is known as *tinkuy*. Not all conflicts are tinkuy: Allen draws a distinction between a ritual encounter and a brawl that she saw erupt between a group of men in the village. The end result of the ritual encounter was tinkuy leading to a sense of unity among the participants. The brawl, on the other hand, was divisive and damaged the social fabric of the community.

Although tinkuy usually refers to ritual encounters, it also has wider applications. The bringing together of different ingredients in cooking to create a taste that is greater than the sum of the spices is tinkuy, as is the bringing together of herbs to create medicine. When two sets of in-laws build a house for a newly wed couple that is tinkuy. When two streams converge in a mass of swirling eddies they are in tinkuy, and such a place is full of uncontrolled spiritual forces that are liberated by (emerge from) the union of the two streams. When a sprouting plant emerges from the earth into the sky, uniting those two different worlds, that is tinkuy as well. The encounter of different energies brings something new into existence, and this something is endowed with a vitalizing life force.

While the tinkuy of ritual combat in the Andes has been suppressed a form of it still lives on in the Andean whipping dances. In these dances people pair up and whip each other's calves with their warak'as (slings). As with the ritual combat, any blood shed is a sacrifice for the Pachamama, who will reciprocate in ayni by providing fertile fields for everyone. When male and female dancers pair up the whipping becomes more ferocious, and something else may enter the picture…"Shall we wander off, little brother? Shall we wander off, little sister? Let's go pick our wakankilla flowers." (From a traditional Andean song sung by men and women during a whipping dance, Allen, pg 156) The couple may slowly disappear into the night, still dancing together.

"The festival of Pukllay is a celebration of life, love, fertility, procreation, and *enqa*, the very life force itself." (Bolin, pg 110). In the dancing and singing…and other activities…that occur during the festival, the Andean people can step outside their normal social constraints, and yet at the same time, these behaviors are channeled in a way that nourishes their culture and their relationship with Nature and the Cosmos. Blood shed is an offering to Pachamama and the Apus, given in ayni for the life they give to the animals and for the fertility they give to the fields. Tinkuy between communities reinforces their separate identities while at the same time uniting them into a union that is greater than the sum of the parts. Young couples who 'wander off' during the dance go on to join in Andean marriage. From tinkuy new life force is released as an emergent property, and all actions are bound by respect for this newly animated life force.

My goal in writing this chapter is to plant the seed of tinkuy in my culture to see what blossoms. The essence of tinkuy, in a nutshell, is the importance of honoring and maintaining differences while at the same time bringing these differences together to form a union. The result of this union of differences is the emergence of new life energy, to be honored and respected as if it were a new Being. "As if it were," is the realm of intent.

The information for this chapter was pulled from:

Allen, C. J. (2002). *The hold life has: Coca and cultural identity in an Andean community (2nd ed.)*. pp 154-156, 174-178.

Bolin, Inge. (1998). *Rituals of Respect: The Secret of Survival in the High Peruvian Andes*. pp 81, 94-100.

ABOUT THOUGHTS

In Western society, our intellect has turned from being our guardian into being our prison guard. (Paraphrase of don Américo Yábar, Carlos Castaneda, and many others).

Don't believe everything you think. (A bumper sticker from www. NorthernSun.com).

I find that I no longer care about philosophy. I'm in love with life...and what I care about is learning how to become a better lover. (Oakley Gordon)

MEDITATION: CONNECTING WITH THE RIVER

Two worldviews (both are valuable in the appropriate context): Ask an engineer and a paqo to define pure water. The engineer may point at distilled water, a liquid that consists of nothing but H_2O. The paqo may point at a spring where it bubbles out of a mountain slope, clear, cold, with dissolved minerals and perhaps bits of plants and insects.*

Go to a river, a river of pure water without industrial pollutants, flowing in its natural river bed. With intent, greet your waiki** (brother/sister/friend) the river. Get in a comfortable position, for in this meditation being comfortable is congruent with what we are about to do. Now, with your intent, open up your energy field and let your filaments commingle with the filaments of the river. Then just relax, let the flowing energy of the river cleanse your energy of any hucha you may have, and let the river teach you how to flow.

When you are finished remember, not out of obligation but out of love, to complete the circle of ayni. Pour a little alcohol into the river, or toss three red and three white flowers into the river, and thank it for being your waiki. The first time I did this the sense I received back was, 'Oh! Wow! Thanks, it's been a long

---

* From a story told to me by don Americo.
** Waiki is an Anglicized version of a Quechua term, please see the glossary for more information.

time since anyone has done that.' and the river sparkled a little more brightly in the light of Tai Tai Inti.

All over the Andes, the people stretch out like lizards on the rocks next to the river, cleaning their energy.

THE MAN WITH
SHINING EYES

One day don Américo and I were driving through the Andes in Pinky Pinky (his red Volkswagen beetle). Américo pulled over and stopped by the side of the road. An old man was sitting there with his back to us, looking out over the valley.

When we drive through the Andes, Américo brings a sack of small loaves of bread to hand out to the salka children we pass in the remote countryside. He handed me a loaf and told me to give it to the old man. I rolled down my window and called out a friendly greeting to him, but the man didn't turn around. I looked back at Américo and he gestured for me to get out of the car. So, I climbed out and walked over and spoke gently to the old man. He turned, gave me a nice smile, accepted the bread, and then without a word turned back to look out over the valley once again. What brought my experience of the world to a momentary standstill were his eyes. They were clear and serene and glistened in the sunlight. When our eyes met, I was brought completely into being there with him, and there was a hint of something very promising about the nature of the Cosmos.

As we drove away Américo told me that he had first noticed the man sitting there ten years earlier, and that since that time he has been there almost every time Américo has driven by. He stops to give the man bread or fruit or a bag of flour or sugar. The man does not come to the car, he accepts the gifts with a smile, and then goes back to looking out over the valley and to the mountains beyond.

When I wrote about this in my Salka Wind blog, I received the following response from a friend of Américo's. "I had a similar visit with an old man of the mountains with don Américo a few years ago. At the time we passed him he was walking along the road and I handed him the bread. I also noted his glistening serene eyes and felt that he was the embodiment of tranquility. Poor in body and possessions, but full in the embodiment of Soul and Spirit. He said, 'Thank you for the bread, but what makes you think I am in need of food. I have the stars to eat,' and he gestured around him."

RIGHT SIDE / LEFT SIDE

The Andean Cosmovision draws distinctions between various aspects of our Being in many overlapping, non-mutually exclusive ways. We have already looked at the three centers of our Being: the llankay, the munay, and the yachay. We have also looked at the three worlds of existence: the uju pacha, kay pacha, and janaq pacha. Now I would like to turn to the distinction between the energy on the right and left sides of our Being.

The energy on our right side (called *paña*) handles our activities in the everyday, ordinary realm of our life, in other words, that aspect of our reality that is created by our society. We tap the abilities of our right side when we work, go to the store, get to our kid's soccer game, balance our checkbook, watch TV, buy airline tickets to go to Peru, and so on. If we want to hold a job, raise children, not get run over when we cross the road, and enjoy our technology, then we need to honor and nourish the energy on the right side of our Being.

The energy on our left side (called *lloqe*) handles our connection to the vast, ineffable mystery that is the Cosmos. The world is so much more beautiful and mysterious—and we are so much more beautiful and mysterious—than we can intellectually conceive. Western society does not acknowledge, does not seem to know about, the nature of our existence beyond the bounds drawn by society itself. The lloqe is our doorway into limitless, unexplored, territory. If we want to know more of who we are and who we can be, and if we want to explore the full potential of our relationship with Nature and the Cosmos, then we can turn to our lloqe.

Our right side and left side are complementary opposite aspects of our Being. We in the West are already facile at working from our right side energy. When we walk the path provided by the Andean Cosmovision we learn how to operate from our left side energy as well. When we know both ways, then yanantin can emerge and we get in touch with that aspect of our Being that is greater than those two parts.

MEDITATION: RIGHT SIDE / LEFT SIDE

All of the Andean meditations activate our lloqe, the energy on our left side. After you have some experience with the Andean meditations and have noticed how they affect your experience of the world and your energy and how you feel, then there is a simple way you can activate your lloqe. Stand with your weight evenly balanced on both feet, then with a hand, or simply in your mind's eye, draw a line down your body from your head to your feet, a line that divides you into your right side and your left side. While doing this, use your intent (sincere pretending) to feel it divide your energy into your right side energy and left side energy. Then, step physically sideways to your left, and with intent step into your left-side energy and its connection to the non-ordinary, vast, mysterious Cosmos. Experience that, then step back to the middle, draw the line gain, and step to the right, using your intent to enter into the energy with which you face your everyday world. Go through the process a few times, getting a sense of the different energies of the two sides.

It may not start off being the difference between night and day. Being on the left side is a learned state that arises from years of experiencing the Andean meditations. This meditation is simply a way of moving quickly into that learned state. Yet still, even if your experience of your lloqe (left side energy) is very tentative, this meditation will shift your energy in that direction.

After you have played with this meditation, you can use it as a lever for shifting your energy when needed. Eventually the physical act of stepping to the right or left can be replaced by pure intent. If you are out under the dome of stars in the night sky for a sacred ceremony and find yourself thinking about what to pick up at the grocery story on the way home, you can use this meditation to shift purposefully into your left side. If you need to drive home and find yourself being spacy from being on the left side, you can shift purposefully to the right. You drive your own bus, that is a lot of what being a paqo/mystic/shaman is all about.

MEDITATION:
SAIWACHAKUY (UPWARD)

This is a meditation I have been enjoying a lot recently. The term *saiwachakuy* as a column of energy was introduced in the earlier meditation Saiwachakuy (Downward). In the meditation we will be looking at in this chapter, the flow of energy moves in the opposite direction, from the Pachamama all the way up past the stars to Mama Tuta.

For this meditation I begin by sitting on the Pachamama, and then I usually do the Touching Pachamama and Releasing Hucha meditations to prepare my energy.

The energy flowing into and out of the Pachamama loves to spiral. With your intent (sincere pretending) open up the energy center at the base of your spine and let the energy of the Pachamama spiral up through your spine and up to and out of the top of your head. With your intent, experience the energy spiraling through your llankay (the energetic center of your physical body located just below your navel) and picking up its energy, then spiraling through your munay (the energetic center of love located in your heart) and picking up its energy, and then spiraling through your yachay (the energetic center of your intellect located in your head), and picking up its energy, and finally spiraling out through the top of your head and up into the Cosmos.

Follow the energy as it spirals up towards the Cosmos. If you are sitting in Nature pause on the way up to connect with and honor the trees and animals and streams around you. Follow the spiraling energy farther up to where it reaches the levels of the Apus (the great Beings who are the majestic mountain peaks) and pause to acknowledge and honor your favorite Apus, one by one, by name. Follow the energy as it continues to spiral higher, up to Mama Killa (the great feminine Being who is our moon) and ask her to connect with and bless your feminine energy. Follow the energy higher until it reaches Tai Tai Inti (the great masculine Being who is our sun) and ask him to connect with and bless your masculine energy. Now follow the column of spiraling energy all the way up to the stars.

We each have our own individual star connected to our llankay (slightly below our navel); honor the star connected to your llankay and ask it to guide your physical body. We have a star connected to our munay (located in the region of our heart); honor that star and ask it to guide your heart. We have a star connected to our yachay (located at the crown of our head), honor that star and ask it to guide your intellect. We have a star connected to the right side of our body; honor that star and ask it to guide you in your everyday life. We have a star connected to the left side of our body; honor that star and ask it to help you keep in touch with the vast, ineffable mystery and beauty of the Cosmos.

And finally, follow the spiral of energy all the way to Mama Tuta, the dark, the void, the night, who holds the stars in her embrace. You may ask her for assistance in walking your path.

Stay for as long as you would like, experiencing this spiraling column of energy and letting it inform your experience of who you are in this incredible Cosmos.

Option One: After you have followed this flow of energy from the Pachamama all the way to Mama Tuta, follow the spiraling energy that flows back down to the Pachamama, completing the circle.

Option Two: I usually don't combine other paths with the Andean one, but I like to incorporate the Eastern chakras into this meditation. As the energy flows up through my base chakra, I have it pick up a band of red color, and through the second chakra a band of orange, and through the third a band of yellow, and through the fourth a band of green, and through the fifth a band of blue, and through the sixth a band of indigo, and through the seventh a band of violet, so that as the spiraling energy emerges through the top of my head it is a rainbow. Then I proceed as described above. My thanks to my friend Karen for suggesting this option.

FILLING IN THE
CONCEPTUAL CORNERS

To the scientist the Andean Cosmovision is a fantasy.
To the paqo the Aristotelian logic of the scientist
is an illusion. (Don Américo Yábar)

In the Andean Cosmovision the Cosmos does not play by the
rules of Aristotelian logic where everything must be either A or
not A. An example of this can be found in the various ways in
which the Andeans conceive the differences between the energies found on the right and left side of our Being.

In an earlier chapter I described how our right side is our
ability to operate in everyday life while our left side connects us
to the ineffable mystery of the Cosmos. I learned this distinction
from don Américo and I have worked with it quite a bit and
have gotten a lot out of it. I have also, however, heard Américo
describe the right side as our "mystical" side and our left side
as our "magical" side. With this distinction our right side represents our ability to comprehend the underlying nature of reality
(mysticism), while our left side represents our ability to influence it (magic).

A third view of the right/left side distinction in the Andes is
provided by the anthropologist Douglas Sharon in his description of the relative roles of the right and left side of the paqo's
mesa (*Shamanism, Mesas, and Cosmologies in the Central Andes*,
2006). A mesa (from the Spanish word for table) is a woven cloth

that serves as a portable altar. A paqo spreads the mesa on the ground or on a flat rock and arranges upon it sacred objects. The objects are placed upon either the right side or the left side of the mesa depending upon their attributes. On the left are placed objects associated with "hot" energy, with the past, with the undoing of energies related to sickness and misfortune. On the right are placed objects associated with "cold" energy, with the future, with the energy of good fortune. The paqo then works from the center of the mesa, transcending both energies.

These various distinctions between the energies of the right and left sides don't necessarily boil down to being different ways of saying the same thing. The right and left side are like this ... and they are also like that ... and they can be like this other thing entirely. This may not be logical, but who (outside of the Western worldview) expects the Cosmos to operate on logical principles? That logic works as well as it does in understanding the Cosmos is due to logic being a product of the same Cosmos it is trying to understand. Logic cannot, however, understand the processes from which logic itself emerged nor can it prove the truth of its own assumptions. The concept that the intellect (and only the intellect) can comprehend the true nature of reality has its basis in both Plato and the Bible; it is one of those assumptions underlying Western culture buried so deeply that it is rarely brought to light to be examine. For a really nice exposition of this I recommend Alan Watts' book *Man, Woman, and Nature.*

CRYSTALLIZATION

As we explore the various facets of our Being: our yachay, munay, and llankay; our right side and our left side; or any of our other facets opened up to us by the Andean Cosmovision, we gain two levels of knowledge. One level of knowledge arises from our exploration of a new facet of ourselves: "Oh, this is what my munay is like!" As we explore these facets over a long period of time, however, a deeper level of knowledge arises. We become more aware of our existence as the diamond that has these facets. Don Américo calls this process our crystallization.

MEDITATION:
INSIDE/OUTSIDE

The Andean path that I have learned from don Américo Yábar has an inherent appreciation for natural balance. There are times, for example, when we want to be fully engaged in the energy of what is going on around us, dancing with it, being influenced by it and influencing it in return. There are also times when we may want to take a break from the dance and withdraw into the sanctuary of our own Being, to be contemplative rather than active, to rest. Here is a simple meditation which gives you that choice.

Begin by standing with your weight evenly balanced on your feet. Notice your present state, how your energy feels, what it is like to be you right now. Then, take one step forward while breathing out and spread your arms in a gesture of opening up your energy field. Do this with the intent (sincere pretending) of letting your energy flow out and connect with the environment around you. Remain in this position long enough to perceive how this affects your experience.

Then, step back while taking an in breath and bring your arms into a shielding position (e.g., cross your forearms on your chest). Do this with the intent of drawing in your energetic connections and creating a protective wall between you and your environment. The flavor of this latter position is not that of putting up a siege barrier*, it is more like that of entering a safe

---

* In a later chapter I will share a process for putting up something that is more like a siege barrier.

haven. Relax within your personal refuge, taking a break from interacting with the energy around you. Spend some time getting in touch with how this affects your experience. Now go back and forth a few times, opening up and going within. If you like the results, then do this occasionally until it becomes part of your repertoire.

The movements and gestures are like training wheels that support the corresponding intent, making the shift obvious and thus easier to learn. You may find that movements other than the ones I described help you to shift into the appropriate state of being. After you have practiced this for a while, the supporting physical movement can become more and more subtle until you can work with intent alone. Judging (using your own criteria) whether it is time to interact with what is going on around you or to take a break, and having the ability to then engage or withdraw, is paqo work. It is a way we can balance taking care of ourselves and taking care of the world around us.

COMING HOME

Diary note: About a month ago I returned home from another trip to Peru where I worked with don Américo and other mystics, paqos, healers, and of course Peru itself. Coming home was hard on me. Perhaps it would be more accurate to say I made it hard on myself. I didn't want to step out of the Andean Cosmovision and back into my Western culture's view of reality. After a couple of weeks of being back—and a fair amount of depression—I finally made the shift. It's not bad, I'm glad I did, and I have learned something by looking back at what I went through during the transition.

My reluctance to return to my Western perspective was based upon fear, a fear that in doing so I would lose what I had gained in Peru and simply return to how I was before I left. Silly me. That is *never* what happens when I return from Peru. What does happen is that I return to my everyday life and to the everyday things I do, I go back to work, I go back to meditating at my favorite spot in the mountains, and then after a while I notice that while I am back I'm not like I used to be. I've changed in a way that leaves me often feeling happier to be on this planet and more enthusiastic to move forward in whatever in the heck it is that I'm doing in this salka dance with the Cosmos (my intellect has little idea and is just along for the ride).

We don't have to go to Peru to have this experience; every time we do one of the Andean meditations we step into salka. It is juicier in Peru, but small steps will get us to the same place as big ones. Whether in Peru or meditating in our backyard, we move into our salka way of being, and then we return to our everyday, domesticated, way of being, and then our Being subtly integrates the two. I've come to realize that this Being, not the Western worldview, not the Andean Cosmovision, is my home. Every time we meditate and then go back to our everyday life we take a tiny step toward home.

When I came back from Peru, I was afraid that re-entering my everyday life would lead to my losing what I had experienced in Peru. The opposite of fear is love.

MEDITATIONS: TAI TAI INTI

The essence of the Andean Cosmovision is to connect with Nature. In this chapter, I would like to share with you how to connect with Tai Tai Inti*, the great Being who is our sun.

Begin by taking a sun shower, stand in the sunlight, let the sunlight flow over you like water. With intent and your hands, wash your outer body and energy in the sunlight as if you are taking a shower. Then, stand facing Tai Tai Inti and let the sunlight flow into your Being through your munay. Be like a flower soaking in the sun. With your intent, let the sunlight spread out from your munay and fill your body until it starts coming out of your pores (you may find that it will take your hucha away with it).

Connecting with Tai Tai Inti in the morning can fill you full of the active energy you need to get through the day: to do chores, go to work, chop wood, and carry water. Connecting with Tai Tai Inti at sunset prepares your energy for entering the evening. The energy of the evening is for moving into the mysteries that reside in the shadows of the night and in our dreams. Connecting with Nature puts us into harmony with the cycles of Nature, which is both beneficial and freeing.

There is also a very special and beautiful meditation that can be performed at sunrise. Go someplace where you can be in Nature to watch the sun rise. Arrive in time to settle down and

---

* Inti is the sun, Tai Tai is a title of greatest formality and respect. Some people refer to Tai Tai Inti as Inti Tai Tai. "I've heard it both ways." (Shawn Spencer)

122

meditate before the sun actually rises. When you sit down, first notice your energy, how it feels to be you. As you are waiting for the sun to appear over the horizon, turn off your internal dialog and let your energy merge with the world around you: the trees, the birds, and particularly the Pachamama. Just be there. As the sun gets nearer and nearer to rising get in touch with the energy of Pachamama as she slowly turns her face to greet the arrival of her loved one. Then, experience the glory and beauty of the arrival of the sun from the first bead of golden light until Tai Tai Inti has risen completely above the horizon (don't stare at the sun of course). When you are finished, notice how the energy of the natural world around you has changed from the time you first sat down. Notice your own energy and how it has changed as well.

THERE I AM!

For a long time I've been going to a special place in the mountains, in the woods, by a creek to meditate. I follow the path of the Andean Cosmovision because at some deep level it resonates in beauty within me, just below the threshold of perception my heart sings, even my intellect smiles and says "I don't understand what is going but I have to admit it's lovely." This keeps me going, even though the momentous moments on the path—when I am thoroughly blown away by my experiences—are few and far between.

The other day I was sitting by the stream with my close friends who are exploring this salka path with me. It was one of those internal dialog days where my mind just didn't seem to want to shut up. We went through a couple of internal-dialog-stopping meditations, and when we finished my internal dialog was quieter but still nattering on. As we sat by the stream and chatted for a while, I found myself withdrawing from the conversation. I was feeling such a strong desire to connect with the river and with the trees on the other side and with the cliff that towers up behind them. As I let my energy, my filaments, connect to the Nature around me, my internal dialog faded away. Then for a brief moment, my experience shifted in a way that is beyond words but led to me exclaiming in a tone of fond affection and pleasant delight, "Oh…there I am!"

MEDITATION: THE CROSS

This special meditation is about the horizontal and vertical aspects of our existence. They intersect at our heart.

I recommend that you prepare your energy and self for this meditation in the usual way. First do the Touching the Pachamama meditation; this will bring your awareness to all of who you are and put you into harmony with the Pachamama, while bringing your various energy centers into harmony with each other. Then you can rid yourself of hucha with the Releasing Hucha meditation. Once in that space, just relax for a bit and be where you are, there is no rush.

Now stand and slowly spread your arms out wide to your sides as if to give the whole Cosmos an embrace. Get in touch with your life here on this planet spread out horizontally in front of you, your triumphs and failures, your joys and despairs, your hopes and disappointments, your optimism and worries, your serenity and your anxieties and your pain, your chores and your delights, the people in your life. Slowly gather all of your life in with your arms in a big embrace and bring it into your heart with your hands. When it enters your heart let your energy flow vertically...when your energy flows vertically you can get in touch with your transcendent self and experience your life from that perspective. Savor the experience for a while. Then, if you wish, repeat the process again, slowly, as many times as you wish.

From your experience, decide if this is something you would like more of in your life. Enjoy.

MEDITATION:
SURFING THE BIG WAVES

This is a meditation I like to do during times when it seems that the Pachamama is going through a lot of changes (earthquakes, hurricanes, landslides, etc). Sit down on the Pachamama, outside in Nature or on the floor of your house, it doesn't matter. Put your hands on the Pachamama. With your intent (sincere pretending), connect with her energy. Let your awareness flow into her. Connect with the flow of the change that is occurring within her. Become one with that flow.

It doesn't get much simpler than this.

THE FLOWER OF EXPERIENCE

Over the years I have gathered quite a collection of notes from my times with Américo. When I am getting ready to teach a salka class, I often review those notes to remind myself of the many and various meditations I have learned from him. Occasionally I run across something he said that is particularly relevant to how I am right now, some quote that I've read dozens of times in the past but this time jumps out as being especially relevant to me right now. I pause when this happens and my energy opens up, blossoms, from within. The next time I read through my notes, the quote is usually again just like all the other quotes, interesting but not highly significant. Below are some of my favorite quotes from Américo. I invite you to come back to this chapter every once in a while and read through them to see if any one of them is particularly what you need to hear today.

Engage in an intuitive exploration of the munay. The love found in the munay is not an emotion, it is the underlying frequency of the Cosmos. The desire of the munay is not for a thing or for a person, it is a desire for being one with the Cosmos.

Interact with the Cosmos with consciousness fully engaged, then the mind will stop running us and instead will come to our service. All of our lives we have been at the mercy of our mind. If we are caught in the net of our thoughts we won't hear the trees talking to us, and we will die thinking about our car.

Investigate life, the flower of experience. Amplify the consciousness and the ecstasy. Investigate the illumination that is energetic (not conceptual or religious). Connect with the internal movement of life, life without ego, a connection with the laws of the Cosmos. Do not be distracted by social and political things, they block the Being of yourself.

Little by little the collective consciousness of the salka groups and other groups on the planet is evolving, and we hope and dream that this energy will be contagious.

The law of teqsemuyu (of the universe) is harmony.
The law of allilaquasay (of life) is to live well, to live well with yourself.

To not know is better than to know; to not know who you really are, or what is really going on, or what it all means, or what will happen next. There are things we know, and things we don't know yet but can know, and then there are those things we can never know. Invite the mystery in. The wind does not know where it is going.

Talk more with the trees, rocks, the wind...and talk less to yourself.

The heart yearns for eternity...and the mind misinterprets that as a desire for permanence.

Reacting mechanically to our world relates us to our habits, our life is mechanical, and pessimism shows up. We look out the windows of our home, sigh, and say "one more day". Open the door to your heart, to the winds of your soul, and you'll say "what a beautiful day". The little girl, who is salka, tending her alpacas and llamas at 15,000 feet on the slopes of the Apu. She is not lonely or bored, she is content, she is joyful, connecting with the rocks, the trees, the animals, the Apus, the wind.

The seed may feel that it is a prisoner in the earth, encased in darkness and confined, but it is being guarded while it germinates.

Love your body as a great mystery.

Time doesn't flow, people flow through time.

This comes from an interview with Américo Yábar in the *Shaman's Drum* (Fall, 1994).

Hal Bennett: *In terms of meeting our global crisis, do you feel going out in this way—to have direct contact with Nature and the Cosmos—is more important than going out and talking with other people?*

Américo: *Yes, yes, absolutely! It is much more important in all aspects: therapeutically, intellectually, spiritually–in all ways. We have to speak to the mountains in the mountains, to communicate with the spirits of Nature in Nature. If you go to the river, the river doesn't lie to you; the river cleanses you. The wind cleanses you. The ancient voices and the spirit of a tree can give you much. These are the only constant and direct presences of the Divine.*

MEDITATION: TRANSFORMING ENERGY

This meditation is somewhat advanced so it would help if you first have a basic understanding of the Andean Cosmovision and have played around with some of the other meditations, particularly those concerning the three centers of Being. This meditation involves transforming our energy. It is simple enough to comprehend intellectually, but what counts is to understand it experientially. You well get a juicier experience if you already have at least a little experience with your three centers of Being (the yachay, munay, and llankay).

Transforming the nature of energy is a part of the path of the Andean paqo. Through the use of intent, it is a surprisingly easy thing to do. We transformed energy, for example, in the simple meditation Saiwachakuy (Downward). If you haven't done that meditation yet, you might want to become familiar with its effects and then come back to this one after you have played around with what it is like to transform energy.

This meditation is an excellent one to dive into when you have too much energy in one of your three centers of Being. In our yachay, this may take the form of not being able to stop thinking about something (obsessing about it) or having our thoughts race around out of control. In our munay, this may take the form of our being all caught up in some whirlpool of emotion and not being able to climb out of it. In our llankay, this may take the form of strong sexual arousal. The goal of this meditation is not to get rid of the energy but instead to take advantage of its presence and strength and play around with transforming it; in doing so we learn more about ourselves...and we become transformed as well.

I will describe how to do this meditation within the context of starting with strong energy in our yachay (for example, not being able to stop thinking about something). It will be easy to then see how to modify the meditation if we are starting with strong energy in our llankay or munay instead.

You can do this either sitting down or standing up, just be sure that you are in a posture where you can easily take quick, deep breaths. It will also help to be sitting or standing comfortably in a vertical position so that the energy can flow up and down your spine in a vertical, rather than a horizontal, direction.

Ok, once you have yourself situated, begin by immersing yourself into the strong energy you have in your yachay. This should be easy as you are doing this meditation because you can't get out of your head in the first place. Attend to how the energy in your head is expressing itself through your thought processes.

Then, with intent coupled with a sharp exhalation, toss that energy down into your munay. Experience how the energy is expressed when it is in your munay. Notice how the energy is different when it is in your munay compared to when it is in your yachay. Immerse yourself for a while in the experience of the energy in your munay. Then, with intent and a sharp inhalation, toss the energy from your munay back up into your yachay. Keep it there long enough to experience again what the energy is like when it is in your yachay.

Next, with intent and a sharp exhalation, toss the energy from your yachay all the way down into your llankay . Experience what the energy is like when it is in your llankay. Immerse yourself in that experience for a while. Then, with a sharp inhalation, toss the energy from your llankay back up into your yachay and notice again what it is like when it is in your yachay.

Finally, with intent coupled with a sharp exhalation, toss the energy from your yachay into your spiritual presence a little ways above your head. Notice how the energy feels when it is expressed in your spiritual realm. Immerse yourself in that experience. To conclude the meditation, you can leave the energy there or move it down into whatever center you want or just keep tossing it around for a while to explore experientially your centers of Being.

Believe me you will not get anything out of this meditation by simply reading about it.

Follow the same basic pattern if you are starting with an excess of emotional energy in your munay or an excess of sexual energy in your llankay. I hasten to add that there is nothing bad about having a lot of intellectual or emotional or sexual energy. This process doesn't get rid of the energy; the energy instead becomes a flying carpet for exploring the other ways we have of being in the world with the volume turned up (to hopelessly mix my metaphors). Wherever you start, toss the energy to one of the other three centers and then back, and then to the other center and back, and finally up to the spiritual realm, and then leave the energy where you choose.

Some thoughts I'd like to share:

* I find this to be a very powerful way to explore the various aspects of my Being.
* It gives me a way to transform my experience without having to deny or fight or resist the excessive energy I may have in one of my centers of Being. It is a loving response to myself.
* Transforming the energy by moving it into a different center of our Being is an act of volition on our part, another way we have of deciding how to dance with the great mystery of the Cosmos and the great mystery of who we are as Beings in this Cosmos. When the energy moves to another center, it transforms us and our experience of that center blossoms a bit more. Are we transforming the energy or is it transforming us?

INTENT REVISITED

In the meditations I define intent as sincere pretending, a very useful definition which I like a lot and that I still use to help guide my experience. This is all you really need to know about intent to engage in and benefit from the meditations and to explore the Cosmos and yourself through the Andean Cosmovision. I have also come to realize, however, that sincere pretending is just the surface of intent and that deep down it is something vastly mysterious and powerful.

The best way I have of describing intent is that as we use the Andean Cosmovision to explore the various facets of ourselves, particularly our munay, we eventually experience our existence as a part of the unified whole of the Cosmos. The farther inside ourselves we go, the bigger we get until we reach the consciousness of the Cosmos itself, and there lies the true origin of our intent. When that pathway is open the consciousness of the Cosmos expresses itself through us; it informs our experiences and our behavior and our understanding of who we are. When we open ourselves to the Cosmos we blossom in the beauty of our unique way of being in this world.

For some people to set intent is to form a goal, to think of a desired outcome. For me, it is getting in touch with the deepest level of my existence and giving it permission to flow out and change me, trusting that the underlying vibrational energy of the Cosmos is love.

MEDITATION: CLEANING HUCHA

As a reminder, hucha is the Quechua term for heavy or chaotic energy. Hucha is a natural byproduct of living in a society where we sometimes need to act in domesticated ways that don't fit our salka nature. Earlier I have shared two meditations for getting rid of hucha in yourself (see Releasing Hucha and Shedding Hucha). Now I would like to share a process for cleaning the hucha from others. As we move to a process that involves working with other people's energy, we appear to stray particularly far from the normal use of the term meditation, but I can think of no closer English term to describe working with energy through intent.

Cleaning the hucha from someone else is one of the important functions of a paqo in Andean society. There are many ways to clean hucha from another person. Some involve the use of quyas (stones with which a paqo has a special relationship) and some involve the use of mesas (a bundle of sacred objects), but the process I would like to share in this chapter is accomplished simply with your intent and your hands and your relationship with Nature and the Cosmos.

Before cleaning the hucha from another person, I first like to get rid of my own hucha using one of the meditations mentioned above. I do this before I work with anyone else's energy to make sure I don't pass any hucha I may have on to them.

This process can be done with your waiki (brother/sister/friend) lying on the Pachamama, but I will describe it in the context of having her or him stand while you do this.

Preliminary step
As you begin, invite your waiki to use his or her own intent to connect with the Pachamama through the feet and with the energy of the Cosmos through the top of the head.

Step 1: Ponqos

a) First prepare your own energy. While standing, raise both your arms above your head with the palms of your hands facing the sky. With intent, connect to the energy of the Cosmos with your right hand and let that energy flow into and accumulate in your right hand. When you feel the energy gathered in your right hand, slowly bring your two palms together (still over your head). When your hands touch, let the energy flow through your right hand into your left hand. From your left hand, let the energy flow down your left arm and into your munay (heart). When the energy flows into your munay, transform that energy into love and let it radiate out from your munay through the rest of your body.

b) Starting at the top of your waiki's head, using both your hands, lightly tap the waiki's body by drumming all of your fingertips on it. Do it as if you are simulating a light rain shower on the body. Your intent, and this is an important piece, is to have each tap create a whirlpool (ponqo) in the waiki's energy body. This loosens up the energy field, making it easier for the waiki to release hucha. Work your way down the front of the body, keeping your taps rapid and light, raising your fingers so they don't quite touch the body when you are over areas that your waiki may not want to have touched. When you get down to the toes repeat the process top to bottom on the back of the body.

Step 2: Cleaning the Physical Body

a) Again prepare your energy. While standing, raise both your arms above your head with the palms of your hands facing the sky. With intent connect to the energy of the Cosmos with your right hand and let that energy flow into and accumulate in your right hand. When you feel that energy gathered into your right hand, slowly bring your two palms together (still over your head) and when they touch, let the energy flow through your right hand into your left hand. From your left hand, let the energy flow down your left arm and into your munay (heart). When the energy flows into your munay, transform that energy into love and let it radiate out from your munay into the rest of your body.

b) Starting at the top of your waiki's head, using both your hands, slowly and lightly draw your fingers down the front of the body, gently touching with your finger tips. Your intent, and again, this is important, is to gather or collect all of the hucha from the physical body with your hands. Keep this intent during the whole process. Do this slowly enough to maintain a clear intent. Work your way down the front of the body, raising your fingers so they don't quite touch when you are over areas that your waiki may not want touched.

c) When you get down to the toes place your hands on the Pachamama and with your intent, ask her to take all the hucha you have gathered in your hands. You may notice that she takes the hucha even as you begin to form the intent to give it to her.

d) Repeat the process (a - c), this time working down the back of the body.

Step 3: Cleaning the Energy Body

a) This is performed exactly like Step 2, but this time you keep your fingers an inch or two away from the physical body and you hold the intent of cleaning the energetic body that emanates from the physical body.

b) Again prepare your energy. While standing, raise both your arms above your head with the palms of your hands facing the sky. With intent, connect to the energy of the Cosmos with your right hand and let that energy flow into and accumulate in your right hand. When you feel that energy gathered into your right hand, slowly bring your two palms together (still over your head) and when they touch, let the energy flow through your right hand into your left hand. From your left hand, let the energy flow down your left arm and into your munay. When the energy flows into your munay, transform that energy into love and let it radiate out from your munay into the rest of your body.

c) Starting at the top of your waiki's head, using both your hands, gently draw your fingers down the front of the body, keeping your fingertips an inch or two from the body. Your intent is to gather or collect all the hucha from the energetic body (which emanates from the physical body) with your hands. Do this slowly enough to maintain a clear intent.

d) When you get down to the toes, place your hands on the Pachamama and with your intent, ask her to take all the hucha you have gathered in your hands.

e) Repeat the process (a – c) this time working down the back of the body.

Step 4: Welcome (Optional)

Give your waiki a hug and welcome him or her to a new state of being.

Step 5: Take Care of Yourself

In general, it is a good idea to take the time after you have worked with someone to rid yourself of any hucha you may have picked up from them. In this particular meditation, however, I have always found that the step of giving their hucha to the Pachamama has taken care of that for me. Still, check out your energy when you are finished. If you feel you have picked up some of their hucha then do one of the getting rid of hucha meditations I have described in earlier chapters.

Options: This can be fun do to in groups of three: one waiki being cleaned of hucha while one waiki works on the front of the body and the other on the back of the body. When finished, switch roles until everyone has had a chance at each position. This also can be done with the waiki lying on the ground and turning over as needed to work on the front and back. Actually, there are lots of other ways of doing this process.

Ponqo. Ponqo is an interesting term with several different interpretations. In this meditation, ponqos refer to small whirlpools of energy that are set up in the waiki's body as you tap. Another use of the term is as a name for the place behind large rocks in a creek where the water forms an eddy, which provides a still point in the current. Fish often take refuge there, resting from coping with the flow of the current. One time when I was in Peru, Américo suggested that when we return to our homes we serve as ponqos for our friends.

THE DELICATE FLOWER

Diary note: I just got back from Peru again, and this is all I can say right now.

There is a delicate flower of freedom within each of us that must be protected and nourished if it is to blossom. Our society does not know of this flower. Nature does. You nourish this flower when you sit next to the river or connect your energy to the stars or fly with the condors, or talk to the Pachamama. (Paraphrase of don Américo).

ON BEING IN PERU

I am a little hesitant to include a picture of my own mug and comment on it in this book—it seems so self-aggrandizing—but here I go anyway. This photo of me is from my 2013 trip to Peru. In the Andean Cosmovision the energy of the left side of our Being is lloqe. It is our connection to the ineffable mystery of the Cosmos. My left eye looks like I am peering into the mystery of the void. The energy of the ride side of our Being is paña, our connection to our everyday life. My right eye is full of love. And my hair, of course, is salka (undomesticated energy). I love being in Peru.

MEDITATION:
THE FOUR ELEMENTS

Our ego consists of all the thoughts and beliefs we have about our Self. A description, however, no matter how detailed, is not the same thing as what it is describing. A description of a strawberry, for example, is not the same thing as a strawberry. All the thoughts we have about who we are, are not the same thing as who we really are. We are much more mysterious than our thoughts can possibly encompass.

For this meditation it helps to be out in Nature. It is not necessary but in my experience it leads to a richer experience.

Begin by using your intent (sincere pretending) to greet the element of Earth (Pachamama). Connect with the Earth, use your intent to ride an out breath and send your filaments into the earth. Experience your filamental connection with the Earth for a while, then bring your awareness to the Earth inside you, for much of our body is made up of elements of the Earth. Don't just think this, experience the Earth within you. With your intent, feel the connection between the Earth upon which you stand and the Earth within yourself.

Next, using your intent, greet the element of water. With an out breath, connect your filaments to the rivers, the lakes, the oceans, the rain. Experience that. Then, bring your awareness to the water inside you, feel the unity of the waters upon the Earth and the water within yourself.

Next, greet the element of fire. With an out breath, connect your filaments to all the fires burning on the planet: the candles, the camp fires, the cooking fires, and the wild fires. Experience that. Bring your awareness to the slow fire within yourself that is your metabolism. Feel the oneness of the fires upon the earth and the fire within yourself.

Next, greet the element of air. With an out breath, connect your filaments to the air around you and any wind or breeze that may be caressing your skin at that moment, then connect to the immense movement of air around this planet. Experience that. Bring your awareness to the air within yourself, flowing in and out of your lungs, and in and out of your bloodstream as it flows to and from all your cells. Feel the unity of the air upon the earth and the air within yourself.

And finally, let your energy expand vertically, down into the ground and up toward the Cosmos, until you become the Tree of Life.

If you only read this meditation you won't get it. It's not about who we think we are nor is it about the *concept* that we are made of the four elements. If you do this meditation, you may experience your Being that is beyond your thoughts. The ego is good, we need our ego to operate in this life, and it is helpful to not get too attached to it. The goal is not to get rid of the ego but to explore who we are beyond it. For this, our ego needs to be willing to stand aside for a while in favor of something even grander.

MEDITATION:
ENERGY SHIELD

In the meditation Inside/Outside I shared a way of disengaging from what is going on around us to retreat into a sanctuary within ourselves. This sanctuary is a place where we can rest from our dance with the world. In that chapter I said that this is not like putting up a siege barrier, it is more like entering a haven where you can recuperate. The meditative-like process I would like to cover in this chapter *is* like putting up a siege barrier, it can be used to protect yourself from unwelcome energy being directed at you from others. This process is meant to be completed before you actually need it.

Begin by picking up a stick or pebble, hold it in your right hand, and put that hand out straight in front of you as if grasping a shield. Now, hold the intent that this stick or pebble radiates a barrier that other energy cannot cross. While holding that intent, rotate your body in the following manner: Keep your left foot where it is in the center of a circle; using your right foot turn you body all the way around in a counter-clockwise direction. Your right foot will be defining the circumference of the circle. As you rotate 360 degrees, keep your hand out with the impeccable intent of this stick or pebble serving as a shield to protect you from outside energy. Go all the way around seven times. This charges the stick or pebble with that intent; you then take it with you where you will need it, and when the time comes, activate the intent again and hold it out as a shield.

The first time I used this process was after I returned home from my second trip to Peru. Particularly for the first few trips to Peru, when I returned home I wanted to hide in the basement for a few days. One of the beautiful things about Peru is that my acceptance by the people there has been based upon my willingness to open my heart to them, and I love them for that. When I come back to the U.S., everyone seems so cold, and particularly because I am a man, being openhearted out in society is not really tolerated or all that safe. When I came home from Peru after my second trip, I knew that the next day I had to attend what was going to be a very hostile faculty meeting. The faculty would be considering a topic that many felt very strongly about; I would be representing one side of the issue, and so some of the hostility would be directed at me. It was like a worse case scenario for an openhearted person who has let down all his barriers.

Before the meeting I went outside and found a pebble and did this process. I put the pebble in my pocket and went to the meeting. As it started, I pulled the pebble out and held it in my fist resting on the table in front of me, and using my intent, I turned it on. It was beautiful. I sat there with what was probably an annoyingly pleasant smile on my face while all the hostility just bounced off or flowed around me. I was able to give my contribution to the discussion without feeling hurt or threatened.

Upon reflection, you might ask, "when would you want to use a stick?" For that, I would like to relate a story that don Américo told when he taught us this process. When Américo was a young man his teacher sent him to spend the night in a cave in the Andes. The cave was the home to a puma, and when the puma returned to find Américo there it wasn't very happy about it. Américo grabbed a stick and went through this process and putting all of his intent into it was able to turn the puma away. When the puma left, Américo tossed the stick aside in relief. A while later, however, the puma returned to have another say in the matter, and Américo found himself scrambling around in the cave before he found the same stick. It is hard to forget a story like that.

My right side is tapping me on the shoulder asking me to add that this was performed by a professional paqo and should not be attempted in a lion cave near your home.

This process is quite different from the others I have shared in that its purpose is to put a barrier between ourselves and some part of the Cosmos. This can be useful, but when possible, I prefer to step around rather then step into situations where I may need it. I have really only had to use it a few times in the almost twenty years since I learned it. The Andean Cosmovision is a way to develop a loving and mutually supportive relationship with ourselves and the rest of the Cosmos. It is not a path of power or domination; its underlying metaphor is not war. It is a path of heart, its underlying metaphors are to explore and to blossom. For all of that, it is not a path for the timid but rather it is a path for the brave, it is risky and scary to open our hearts to the world, for along with the uttermost joy, we may find great pain. It calls for the courage and impeccability of a warrior, but we are warriors of the heart. The true confrontation is to stand naked in front of the incredible power and mystery of the Cosmos and ask if it would like to dance.

MEDITATION:
CONFESSING TO NATURE

If you have something you need to confess, to get off your chest, go to Nature and confess it out loud to a tree or to a stream or to a bird or a cliff or to Tai Tai Inti or to Pachamama. By itself, I don't know if this would make a big difference in your life, but as part of your changing relationship with Nature and the Cosmos it is a small but beautiful step. After many of these small steps, you will begin to notice a change in yourself that arises from a change in the quality of your relationship with Nature.

By the way, when don Américo was suggesting this to us he also mentioned in passing that we are allowed to make the exact same mistake in our lives three times before we have to start feeling like an idiot. I hope you read this chapter during the international "cut yourself some slack week".

PEELING THE ONION

Many, many years ago, when I first started down a spiritual path, I thought it would be a path of slowly increasing bliss. When I tell that to people now we all sit back and laugh. Instead what I found is that I had a lot of encrustation to get rid off, gunk (to use a polite term) that I had picked up in my life, decisions I had made about how to approach life that led to pain and depression, beliefs that I had adopted from family and friends and society and then incorporated into my personal identity even though they weren't mine, unhelpful assumptions about what I can and cannot do, should and should not do, be and should not be. The path for me has been one of working my way through all of that in search of the experience of the essence of who I really am and of my true relationship with the Cosmos.

I don't know any way to get beyond those issues other than to go through them, and the process can be painful as I face aspects of my ego that I do not like or episodes in my life that I suppressed rather than resolved. The result of successfully moving through an issue, however, leads to joy and a sense of liberation and a step closer to who I really am. This is what keeps me going. Then, the next issue arises and the pain and/or depression returns until I move past that. Sometimes it seems that an old issue surfaces again and again and I despair that I will never get past it. But in looking back over the years I can see that when I feel like I am facing yet again an issue I've worked on many times before, it is more like I am in a spiral, and as I come across it again it is from a higher spot. What I learn this time takes me closer to an aware-ness of who I really am.

To paraphrase Américo: We are like onions, we keep peel-ing away one layer after another to finally get to the center. And, when we get to the center, we find nothing....we find we are no thing.

ALTO MESAYOQ

In the Andean tradition an *alto mesayoq* is a very high level paqo. They are usually described in the shamanistic literature as powerful paqos with incredible abilities, but I think that description misses a major point. While we were in Peru last summer, my friend Karen asked Gayle Yábar (don Américo's son and a great paqo himself) to tell us about the alto mesayoqs. He paused and then replied that alto mesayoqs were paqos who spent their whole lives in service to an Apu.

Later we had lunch...and as usual...Gayle served us our food.

CONNECTING WITH PACHAMAMA

Almost very meditation we have covered involves connecting with the Pachamama. There is something, however, that I would like to share that is not really a meditation on its own but is something that may serve you well.

There are some meditations, both in the Andean Cosmovision and in other traditions, that take our consciousness way out there. Before embarking on such a journey, spend a moment connecting to the Pachamama. Using your intent ask the Pachamama to connect her filaments to your filaments as an anchor that will remain while you soar. This makes it easier to come all the way back when you have finished your journey. Isn't she loving?

HOW TO PROCEED

Walking the path of the Andean Cosmovision will bring you to the world of salka (your undomesticated energy). Previously unknown aspects of yourself and of the Cosmos will slowly unfold for you to explore. Your relationship with Nature and the Cosmos will change, and whenever a relationship changes, the relata (the elements that are in relationship) change as well. That part of your Being that appreciates beauty and values love will begin to hum a fetching tune, and so will Nature and the Cosmos.

To walk this path, you do not need to believe any specific set of beliefs. Actually you need to unbelieve some things, including the belief that any beliefs about reality have much to do with reality itself. Your mind will evolve from being your prison guard to being your ally in an exploration of a Cosmos that is more mysterious and wonderful than your thoughts can possibly encompass.

My first suggestion on how to proceed is to connect with the Pachamama every day using the Touching the Pachamama meditation.* This takes only a couple of minutes, really, there is room for this in our daily lives. Complete the circle of ayni with the Pachamama by expressing your gratitude to her and through occasional, simple despachos. This is enough, this is walking the

---

* Not every day. If something is done every day it can become mechanical, a rite that loses its connection to what it can evoke. On the other hand, the long-term benefits of this will arise only if it is done a lot, on a regular basis, and begins to inform how you approach your life. A ray of sunlight every few weeks will not allow the flower to blossom.

path of the Andean Cosmovision, you will change. Many small steps will eventually take you far. And...there is also more to explore if you desire.

There is a lot to be said for getting rid of our hucha on a regular basis. It leads to a much pleasanter life. Do the Releasing Hucha meditation after the Touching the Pachamama meditation. Again, this takes just a minute or two. Remember to do your part in the dance of ayni with the Pachamama, giving back to her for her willingness to take your hucha and recycle it into refined energy. It is an act of love from her. And there is more to explore if you desire.

If you find you like this path then try all the various meditations at least a few times to get a sense of their effect on you. Rely on your own deep sense of what is good and beautiful and loving, and evaluate each meditation from that place. Add the ones you like to your repertoire of ways to face the mystery of your existence. When you meditate, pick the one that feels right for you today.

There are times to be feminine and times to be masculine; times to be your own mother and times to be your own father; times to operate from your intellect, times to operate from your heart, and times to operate from your body; there are times to engage in the dance and times to withdraw; and there are times to operate from your right side and interact with society and times to operate from your left side and connect with the vast ineffable Cosmos. You are not these various facets of your diamond; you are the diamond. The more you explore your facets the more the diamond aspect of your Being emerges into your awareness.

But it is all out there beyond words. Words serve as scaffolding that help us build the experience that is available in each meditation. When the scaffolding has done its job, you can take it down and start living in the house you have created.

GLOSSARY

The following are the Quechua terms used in this book with the addition of some other terms that you may encounter when studying the Andean Cosmovision. Quechua is the indigenous language of the Andes and is still widely spoken in the more remote villages of Peru. Written Quechua is essentially an attempt to recreate the sounds phonetically in Spanish. Several attempts have been made over the years to come up with an official way to write Quechua but several variations are still used. I have selected a form that helps me to pronounce the words more or less correctly. Again, the letters are pronounced as if the language were Spanish.

You will notice the use of apostrophes, as in *paq'o* or *Q'ero*. The apostrophe represents a glottal stop (a strong click in the throat). You are likely to be understood, however, even if you can't pull that off. And, in my writing I often don't bother to include the apostrophes and simply write paqo rather than paq'o, Qero rather than Q'ero, and so on.

The sound of the following pairs of letters makes sense if you consider them to be a sequence of two sounds, the first being the Spanish pronunciation of the vowel and the second one being an English long "e" sound.

"ay" rhymes with English "tie"

"uy" sounds like "we"

TERMS

alto mesayoq: the higher of the two commonly recognized levels of being a paqo (the other is pampa mesayoq).

apocheta: a doorway into another energy, also a cairn of stones on the shoulder of an Apu.

Apu: a great spiritual Being who is a majestic mountain peak.

ayllu: an ancient Quechua term not defined in the same way throughout the Peruvian Andes: in general it is a community defined by being kin, by being together geographically, or by sharing a common focus.

ayni: the principle of reciprocity.

chakra: a small cultivated field (a daughter of Pachamama).

chullpa: a type of small stone tower found in the Andes; in some stories it is a tomb or home of the Machukuna (the ancient ones, the children of the moon).

despacho (Spanish origin): an offering, often made to the Pachamama or the Apus or some other Being of the Cosmos.

haywarisca: a Quechua term for a despacho of gratitude.

janaq pacha: one of the three levels of reality (along with the kay pacha and uju pacha), it is the consciousness of the superior or upper world and the future.

hucha: heavy, chaotic energy. We naturally pick up hucha as we live in our society.

kay pacha: one of the three levels of reality (along with the janaq pacha and uju pacha), it is the consciousness of the surface world, where we live our lives, and it is also the present time.

k'intu: a bouquet of three coca leaves, held at the fingertips. Your blow your filaments into the k'intu as part of a sacred ceremony.

llankay: one of the three centers of our Being (along with the munay and yachay). It is the center of our physical body and our ability to bring things into manifestation. The llankay is located a few finger breadths below the navel and a couple of inches inside the body.

Machukuna: the ancient ones (the children of the moon).

mesa (Spanish for "table"): a woven cloth that is used to carry sacred objects such as quyas. The mesa is spread out on a rock or on the ground to provide a platform upon which the sacred objects are arranged as part of a ceremony.

munay: one of the three centers of our Being (along with the llankay and yachay). It is where we can sense our connection with the Cosmos and feel the underlying vibrational frequency of the Cosmic filaments, which is love. The munay is located in the region of our heart.

pacha: a term that combines space, time, and consciousness.

pachacuti: a space/time/consciousness of monumental cosmic transformation. The term also refers to one of the Inca rulers, Pachakuti (Pachakuteq) Inca Yupanqui, who ushered in an era of great change.

Pachamama: the great Being who is our mother the planet Earth.

pampa mesayoq: the lower of the two commonly recognized levels of being a paqo (the other being the alto mesayoq).

paq'o: Andean mystic, shaman, healer, diviner.

phukuy: the act of gently blowing your filaments through a k'intu, usually with the intent of connecting your finest energies and those of the coca with the energies of the Pachamama, the Apus, and your community.

Q'ero: an isolated region in the high Andes of Peru and the people who live there.

q'uncha: an earth stove, a hollow mound of clay/earth with an opening on the side to feed the fire and holes on the top for pots to sit in. It is considered to be the heart of the wasitira.

q'uya: a special stone with which you develop a special relationship.

Runakuna: The indigenous people of the Andes.

salka: undomesticated energy.

salka wasi: don Américo's house in the high Andes, the "house of undomesticated energy".

uju pacha: one of the three levels of reality (along with the kay pacha and janak pacha), it is the consciousness of the lower or interior world and the past.

yachay: one of the three centers of our Being (along with the munay and llankay). It is the center of the intellect from which our thoughts arise. It is located in the crown of our head.

yanantin: the complementarity of opposites. For example, the bringing together into harmony of male and female energy.

waiki: an Anglicized version of a Quechua term for what a male calls his brother. Don Américo Yábar uses this term as an affectionate way to refer to friends of both sexes and it has come to convey such a sense of acceptance and affection and good humor that its use has become widespread among those who know him.

wak'a: a sacred site.

warak'a: a woven sling used to throw stones, it also serves as a whip.

warmi-qhari: (literally woman-man) the fusion by marriage of two different but interdependent beings, female and male, with their complementary skills and interests, into a unified whole from which something greater than the sum of the parts emerges.

wasi: house.

wasitira: an adobe house (literally "house-earth") formed out of the living Earth. An adobe house is an extension of the Pachamama, and thus people who live in a wasitira live inside the Pachamama herself.

RECOMMENDED READING

BOOKS ABOUT THE PEOPLE OF THE ANDES

Masters of the Living Energy: The Mystical World of the Q'ero of Peru. Joan Wilcox. Inner Traditions Press. 2004. This is an excellent presentation on the ideology and practices of the Q'ero paqos, written with the carefulness of a scholarly work but without the insistence on the preeminence of the Western world view that is usually found in academia.

Rituals of Respect: The Secret of Survival in the High Peruvian Andes. Inge Bolin. University of Texas Press. 1998. This is a beautiful book written by an anthropologist who lived for some time with the Chillihuani people in the high Andes. While Joan's book has much more information about the paqos, Inge's book gives a much deeper look into the culture and the lives of the people.

The Hold Life Has: Coca and Cultural Identity in an Andean Community (2nd Ed.). Catherine J. Allen. Smithsonian Books. 2002. This book, like Inge's, provides a window into the lives of the Andean people. In this case the community is somewhat lower in the mountains and less isolated than the Chillihuani (and to me at least has a little less magic and beauty) but I felt the book helped fill in the corners of my understanding of Andean culture in important ways, particularly in respect to the crucial role of coca in the people's lives.

"Shamanism, Mesas, and Cosmologies in the Central Andes". Douglas Sharon. In *Mesas & Cosmologies in the Central Andes.* San Diego Museum of Man. 2006. Purely academic but it has some gems in it.

RELATED MATERIALS
The following, while not specifically about the Andean Cosmovision, have helped me bridge the gap between the world-view
of my culture and that of the Andes. They are also just really
good reads.

"The Ecology of Magic", a chapter by David Abram in the book
Ecopsychology (T. Roszak, M. E. Gomes & A. D. Kanner, Eds.),
Sierra Club Books. 1995. This is a great academic description
of the type of mysticism found in the Andes (even though the
author is writing about his experiences in Bali).

"The Bird and the Machine", a chapter in Loren Eiseley's *The
Immense Journey: An Imaginative Naturalist Explores the Mysteries of
Man and Nature*, Vintage Press. 1959. This is a beautiful narrative
about nature, science, the intellect, and the heart. It is worth
tracking down and reading, I think you'll love it. Really.

Nature, Man, and Woman, by Alan Watts. Vintage Press. 1991. Alan
Watts is a wonderful author. His books about Taoism, Buddhism,
and other similar topics had a big influence on me when I was a
young man. In this book, I particularly recommend the first 70
pages in which he lays out some important concepts concerning
the relationship between Western science, Western religion, and
our thinking about the nature of Nature. The book is a bit dry
after that (in my opinion).

A New Earth: Awakening to Your Life's Purpose, by Eckhart Tolle.
2005. Plume. An excellent book about stopping the internal dialog and not doing. There are several ways in which this book
dovetails with the Andean Cosmovision, including the connection between our conscious experience and nature.

ACKNOWLEDGEMENTS

This book is proof that my family loves me and wants me to be happy. Thank you Betsy, Ben, and Christopher.

Of the people in Peru there are, of course, Américo Yábar and his son Gayle Yábar who have opened the door to the Andean Cosmovision for me and have guided me along the path. Américo's daughter, Arilu, has put so much work into insuring that I am safe and taken care of in Peru. At Salka Wasi I would like to thank doña Maria and don Abolino, and don Miguelito who have healed me, fed me, and guided me on my path. There are so many men and women of Peru who have given me karpays and despachos. Those whose faces I see most clearly as I write this are the late don Pascual, don Fabion, and don Domingo, and the still living don Bonito, don Pascualito, and don Martin.

And then there is Peru itself. Its places of power have altered my Being. I would like to give a special acknowledgement to Salka Wasi as well as to Apus Ausungate, Salkantay, Pachatusan, Jamanlipa, and Ñusta Veronica.

Although we all walk our own paths I do love the company of wonderful friends. Three waikis (friends) in particular have been walking arm-in-arm with me down this path for years and have been a tremendous support to me as well as a source of laughter and light: Karen Cottingham, Curtis Forbush, and Angela Rhinehart.

Barbara Mahan took on the huge task of editing the text for me. Thank you so much Barbara. The book design came from Becky Fulker.

And finally, I would feel remiss if I didn't mention the Blue Star Cafe, Sugar House Coffee, Whispers Cafe, and Beans & Brew. I deem it unlikely that I will ever earn enough money from this book to cover the lattes that went into writing it (but I got a lot of good lattes out of it).

ABOUT THE AUTHOR

My name is Oakley E. Gordon. Many years ago, when I was an undergraduate college student, I became interested in the psychology of consciousness. This led me into the exploration of a variety of Western and Eastern approaches to the study of consciousness: Zen, Taoism, Sufism, Gestalt therapy, and the writings of Alan Watts, John Lilly, Robert Ornstein, Charles Tart, and Carlos Castaneda (among others). When I decided to enter graduate school, I searched for a sub-discipline of psychology that would fit my interests and eventually earned a Ph.D. in cognitive psychology (the scientific study of perception, memory, learning, and consciousness). This path led to a melding of my interest in consciousness, my penchant for science, and my love of teaching. While cognitive psychology has provided me with a career as a professor of psychology, my core interest in the nature of consciousness eventually led me to the Andean Cosmovision, which has taken my studies beyond the confines of academia, beyond the scope of science, and ultimately beyond the view of reality held by Western society.

In 1994, I met don Américo Yábar of Peru and he invited me to become his student. That was the beginning of what has now been 20 years of going to Peru to study with him and with the paqos he has arranged for me to meet, to be with the people of Peru, and to be with Peru itself. All of these have had a tremendous effect on me.

While I learned how to explore the Andean Cosmovision in Peru, most of the actual exploration has taken place when

I have been back home in the United States. I have faced several challenges along the way. The first challenge was to learn how to leave my Western view of reality behind and enter into a completely different way of experiencing and interacting with the Cosmos. The second challenge was to figure out how to integrate my experiences with the Andean Cosmovision into my life here in the West. And the third challenge has been to figure out how to teach this all to others in my culture. These have all been interwoven. Over the years of going to Peru, coming home to make sense out of what I have experienced, and teaching what I have learned to others, I have come to the point where I could write this book. I offer it to you from my munay (with help from my yankay and llachay).

My website dedicated to salka and the Andean Cosmovision can be found at: www.SalkaWind.com

45842961R00098

Made in the USA
Lexington, KY
13 October 2015